Don't Trust the Abbot

Musings from the Monastery

Abbot Jerome Kodell

LITURGICAL PRESS
Collegeville, Minnesota

www.litpress.org

1	2	3	4	5	6	7	8	9

Library of Congress Cataloging-in-Publication Data

Kodell, Jerome.
    Don't trust the abbot : musings from the monastery / Jerome Kodell.
      p. cm.
    ISBN 978-0-8146-3238-3 (pbk.)
      1. Spirituality—Catholic Church.   I. Title.
  BX2350.65.K63 2009
  248.4'82—dc22

                                             2008047558

For Sister Mary Agnes, Cleo, and Anna

Contents

Introduction   vii

Trust and Faith: Jesus Is the Way

Call It Trust   3
Don't Trust the Abbot   5
The Meeting Tent   7
God's Mantra   10
The Silence of Mary   12
Watch the Signs   15
Sabbath   17
Truth Is Beauty   19
Caught between Accepting and Choosing   21
I Am Invisible   23
Celibacy   26

Christian Life: With and In Community

The God of Hearsay   31
Coldhearted Orthodoxy   33
The Covenant of Salt   35
Prosperity Theology   37
The Christian Reflex   39
Over-responsibility   42
A Lesson from the Desert   44
The Turtle on the Fencepost   46

Halos and Dark Nights   48
The Surprise of Mother Teresa   50
A Monastic Doctor of the Church   52
Mary and Peter in the Church   55
The Disciple and the Mother   57
Empowered by the Word of God   60
Joy in Honduras   62
The Gift of the Resurrection   64

Prayer: To See as God Sees
Holy Seeing   69
God's DVD Library   71
Distractions in Prayer   73
A Communion of Intercession   75
Golden Prayer   78
The Usefulness of Monasteries   81
Why Monasticism?   83
The Family of Jesus   86
Private Revelations   88
A Rock to Cling To   90
The American Dream   92

Introduction

One day when I was working in the library at Subiaco Abbey's mission monastery in Belize, Central America, a little girl came in looking for a book. I was happy to see the interest in reading and stood up to help her. I asked her what kind of book she would like. "A big one," she said. "I need something to stand on."

This little book, I'm afraid, will not be much use in trying to reach the top shelf, but I've found that small books are more likely to be read than large ones, even though they may not be nearly as important. Small books don't look so scary, and you can carry them around in a pack or purse. And the size of the book doesn't determine the size of the topic.

This book is about a number of different topics but they all deal with one main subject, our life with God and our search for God, whether individually or with others. It is a collection of my articles from Subiaco Abbey's newsletter, *The Abbey Message*, spanning the time that I have been abbot, 1989–2008.

As is customary in most monasteries, each issue of the newsletter contains some kind of communication from the superior sharing news or expressing the spirituality and vision of the community. At the time of my election, *The Abbey Message* appeared six times a year, but in 1994 it became the quarterly it remains today. By now I have written nearly eighty articles in the newsletter as abbot.

Over these nineteen years, some articles have aroused a response while others have barely been noticed. There was an especially strong interest in three articles on prayer published in consecutive issues in 1996 and 1997, and as a result that series was developed into a booklet, *Twelve Keys to Prayer*, published by Liturgical Press in 1999.

I didn't have any plans for wider circulation of the other newsletter articles until I began to receive requests from three readers in Texas, who eventually put a great deal of time and effort into retrieving the articles from past issues and suggesting various plans about selecting, organizing, and publishing. Their interest and their generous work on my behalf got my attention and I began to work with them, eventually selecting about half the newsletter articles for the present collection of *Don't Trust the Abbot*.

I am very grateful to my three coworkers, to whom I am dedicating this book. They gave the impetus and did much of the work and deserve a big share of the credit for any help new readers of these articles may receive for their spiritual journey.

Trust and Faith: Jesus Is the Way

Call It Trust

In spiritual conversations among Christians, before too long the word "faith" is likely to come up. The gift of faith is prerequisite for becoming a Christian. The church is made up of "the believers" and calls itself the "community of faith."

It was a dispute about faith that split the church at the time of the Protestant Reformation. Are we saved by faith alone, or by faith and works? We know now that the dilemma was a false one; both Catholics and Protestants agree that true faith "work[s] through love" (Gal 5:6) in opening us up to saving grace: "by grace you have been saved through faith" (Eph 2:8). But the consequence of the misunderstanding underscores the seriousness of the issue.

We still find it hard to define the meaning of faith. From the New Testament on, Christian faith has been capable of many nuances. The positive side of that is richness of meaning; the negative side is vagueness and imprecision. Faith means one thing in the admonition "Know your faith," another in the statement "My faith is weak." What does it mean to grow in faith (see 2 Cor 10:15)? What kind of faith is meant in the expression "Believe and you will be saved"? For Catholics, the word "faith" often implies a doctrinal content. We don't just believe; rather we believe something about someone and what that means for us. We have a Creed, which we use to profess our faith every Sunday.

Applying this broader understanding of faith to the questions in the preceding paragraph, a weak faith would indicate poor instruction or a lack of conviction about the truths in the Creed, and to grow in faith might mean to increase our study time and pray for stronger conviction.

The fact is that only one of the phrases above refers to doctrine: "Know your faith." In the other cases faith means "trust"—not

3

trust in a doctrine or belief but trust in a person: God the Father or Jesus, his son.

Faith as believing in something is secondary to faith as believing in someone. I think that the word "trust" is often more helpful than "faith" in expressing the primary New Testament meaning of faith, the fundamental attitude that opens us to peace and salvation. We may differ individually in our grasp of the details of revealed doctrine, but we all know what it means to trust another person. The call of the Gospel is to let go of our self-protection and anxieties and to give our lives over in trust to Jesus.

This is precisely the test. In the midst of the problems and dilemmas of my daily life, can I believe that there is really a God who knows what is going on, who cares about me and loves me? This is not the question of the existence of God. I may believe in God without trusting God. I may believe in the existence of a creator and judge for the whole world, without being convinced that this God is present in my life moment by moment, watching over me and loving me in the midst of my pains, doubts, tragedies, and loneliness.

Yet that is what it means to believe. It is the trust of Abraham, who left his known surroundings at the call of God, without a clue to his destination. It is the trust of Moses, who stood before the Red Sea with Pharaoh's army bearing down on him with nothing to hang on to except the promise of God, "I will be with you." Saint John of the Cross expressed this with the telling phrase, "O guiding Night."

Peace comes from trust. We are under the illusion that peace comes from knowledge of the future and secure provision for the future. Deep down we know this is a false hope. We will never know the future, only the present and the past; and we will never be able to provide absolute security for ourselves, no matter how rich or powerful we may be. Eventually disease, heartache, the diminishments of age, or calamity will break through our defenses—or if none of the above, eventually death. Ignorance of the future, one of the saints has said, is the greatest unrecognized blessing of God.

At the Last Supper, Jesus told the disciples that he was going away to prepare a place for them in the Father's house. He assured them, "Where [I] am going you know the way." This was astonishing news. "Master," said Thomas, "we do not know where you are going; how can we know the way?" Jesus told him: "I am the way" (John 14:3-6).

This seemingly obscure answer is right to the point. The way to heaven is not a paved road or even a mapped road. It is a path that opens up in the darkness as we go forward, walking with Jesus. We do not need to know where Jesus is going. It is enough that he knows and that he takes us with him. Jesus promised to be with us every step of the journey (Matt 28:20). The faith that saves us is trust that Jesus can be taken at his word.

Don't Trust the Abbot

It is one thing to trust God and Jesus as the Son of God as faithful guides on the way to eternal life, but it is something else entirely to trust the people who exercise authority in God's name. There is no way around this dilemma, because God's plan of redemption is incarnation, that is, salvation mediated through human beings, beginning with Jesus Christ. Authentic Christianity requires obeying the human authorities duly appointed. How do we know that we can trust these weak human beings to lead us faithfully to God?

Saint Benedict addresses this question in chapter 4 of his Rule, "The Tools of Good Works," a manual of six dozen admonitions for successful living of the monastic life. He took this chapter almost verbatim from an earlier source, the Rule of the Master, but he edits a few maxims and adds a handful of his own. The one that he has edited most elaborately is verse 61, which was in his source as "Obey the orders of the abbot." Benedict expands it as follows: "Obey the orders of the abbot in all things, even if his own conduct—which God forbid—be at odds with what he says. Remember the teaching of the Lord: 'Do what they say, not what they do.'"

Benedict is applying to the monk's life a comment of Jesus about the abuse of authority by Jewish leaders in his time: "The scribes and Pharisees have taken their seat on the chair of Moses. Therefore, do and observe all things whatsoever they tell you, but do not follow their example. For they preach but they do not practice" (Matt 23:2-3). The leaders are legitimately "on the chair of Moses," and so their directives can be safely followed, even if their own conduct does not live up to what they teach. Jesus is not referring here to directives that are immoral, unethical, or against the faith. He is not advocating "blind obedience." A faithful disciple may not obey such commands no matter who gives them. Jesus is talking about the legitimate exercise of religious authority. This is a great protection for the disciple. Obedience to the legitimate religious authority is obedience to God no matter who holds the office, saint or sinner. But on the other hand, the bad example of the superior is no excuse for the disciple.

In this way, Benedict relieves the monk of the wrong kind of respect for the abbot while preserving the abbatial authority that sanctifies the monk's obedience. It is dangerous to trust the abbot and other religious authorities too much, because when they slip, as all humans do, it may seem that the whole enterprise is going down. But the sinfulness and errors of those in authority do not invalidate the authority. Jesus does not say we have to trust the one in authority whom we obey. Hopefully the leader will earn our trust by faithfulness and good example, and that improves the experience of obedience dramatically. But it is not necessary to trust the religious authority in order to obey and to receive the blessings of obedience.

Problems arise when people fail to make the distinction between trust in and obedience to religious authorities. Since 2002, the media has carried many stories of Catholics who have left the church because of the failure of some bishops to respond honestly and appropriately to the clergy abuse scandal. We know that through history monks have left monasteries sometimes solely because of the poor leadership or sinful conduct of abbots. Laity have left the church because of pastors.

But we are not required to trust our religious leaders unless they earn our trust by their conduct. The requirement for salvation is faith, which means trust in God. Applied to the church and religious life, this means we are called to trust in God to carry out the divine plan and purpose for the church and its members through whatever human leaders God happens to have placed in charge.

Saint Benedict foresaw that some abbots might be saints and others might be scoundrels, and that bad abbots could create anxiety among their subjects. But he is reassuring: if you obey those God has placed in authority you will be obeying God, and God will sanctify you. In other words, he presents God as saying: You don't have to trust anyone but me—not the abbot, not the bishops, not even the pope. You need to obey them in the legitimate exercise of their office, and to trust them when you can. The obedience will make you a saint, no matter what they do. I can work out my plans, whoever is in charge on earth. It may not be pretty, but it will be effective. Trust me.

The Meeting Tent

As the pilgrim people of God made their way through the wilderness on the way to the Promised Land, at every stage Moses would set up a meeting tent outside the camp. This was not a tent for public meetings, as the name might imply, but a place to encounter God: "Anyone who wished to consult the LORD would go to this meeting tent outside the camp" (Exod 33:7).

Though anyone could go to the tent, it was critical to the journey that Moses, the leader, should visit the Lord in the tent, and so all eyes were on him: "Whenever Moses went out to the tent, the people would all rise and stand at the entrance of their own tents, watching Moses until he entered the tent" (Exod 33:8). When they saw the column of cloud descend to the tent, they knew Moses was conversing with God, and seeing this, all the people would worship at their own tents.

The way through the wilderness was uncharted. The people knew that they would make it through only by the guidance of God, and therefore it was vital to their interests that the leader stay in contact with God. Moses did not know the way, and he did not have to, as long as he stayed close to God.

This is always the pattern of spiritual leadership. The journey to the Promised Land is always in the wilderness, and no human leader knows the way. It is not the job of the leader to know the way, but to stay in contact with God, who does know the way. The main responsibility of a spiritual leader—the pope, a bishop, a religious superior, a pastor—is to go to the meeting tent to be with God every day. The people do not expect their leaders in the faith to know everything, and they become concerned when leaders think they do. What gives people confidence is that the leader is close to God. This doesn't put an end to the errors of human weakness, but it protects from losing the way.

The gospels tell us that the key ingredient to discipleship is faith: "Your faith has been your salvation." This is not just any faith, such as believing the truth of the teaching, but faith in its personal meaning as trust. Salvation comes from putting our trust in God and in his son Jesus. Growth in knowledge of the faith comes from study, but growth in trust comes only from personal contact—prayer—with God. We are not asked to put our trust in human leaders, but in God. The closer our leaders are to God, the more at home they are in his tent, and the more we can put our trust also in them.

Everyone, not just leaders, is called to intimacy with God. But it is easier for people to seek a close relationship with the Lord themselves if they know their leader is praying. "As Moses entered the tent, the column of cloud would come down and stand at its entrance while the LORD spoke with Moses. On seeing the column of cloud stand at the entrance of the tent, all the people would rise and worship at the entrance of their own tents" (Exod 33:9-10).

Something happened to Moses when he went into God's presence, something he seemed to be the last to notice. When he came down from Mount Sinai after being with God for forty days, the people noticed that his face had become radiant, an outward sign of something happening within. The same thing happened to Jesus on Mount Tabor at the transfiguration (Luke 9:29). The inner transformation this represents is offered to all who spend time with God in the meeting tent. In the Latin Bible, the meeting tent is *tabernaculum*, the source of our word tabernacle, which the church very appropriately adopted as the name for the place of the Blessed Sacrament. The meeting tent with God can be pitched anywhere in our lives, but the tent of the Blessed Sacrament, a permanent witness to the Eucharist we have shared, is a privileged place to spend time in the divine presence.

The meeting tent of Moses gives one means of access to understanding the place of religious life in the church. Religious life is to be a sign or emphasis of a particular part of the spiritual journey that is true for every disciple. Yet all of us are called to holiness, all are called into intimacy with God, all are called to the tent every day. Some are invited to do this as a sign to the church, to be as Moses was for the people in the wilderness, a hopeful reminder that God is with us on the way. Religious (those who are members of religious orders) don't do this instead of others, and they don't necessarily do it better. But their life is a sign of hope. The other members of the Body of Christ want religious to be holy and to pray, not instead of them but with them, keeping their eyes "fixed on Jesus" (Heb 12:2) as a reminder and encouragement for all to do the same. It should come as no surprise that religious communities, with their antennae up, are often among the first to sense and to respond to a new need or new opportunity in the church and in the world, a new direction in the wilderness. What are they to do about it? Only time in the presence of God will reveal the answer to that.

There is "one thing necessary," and when the journey is over, what will have made the difference for the religious is whether or not he or she has gone faithfully to the tent. And it is the same for all of us.

God's Mantra

A mantra is a short word or phrase used repetitively in prayer. We still sometimes call such phrases ejaculations— "My Jesus, mercy"; "Jesus, Mary, Joseph"—but the word "mantra," borrowed from the Eastern religions, indicates a particular way of using such phrases. They are repeated over and over again as a way of maintaining focus on God during a time of contemplative prayer.

In Christian usage phrases such as those above ordinarily express devotion or state a faith conviction or hope. Other favorites are "Maranatha" (1 Cor 16:22; either in the original Aramaic or in translation as "Come, Lord Jesus"), the Jesus Prayer ("Lord Jesus Christ, have mercy on me, a sinner"), or simply the name of Jesus. The Hail Marys of the rosary are a kind of mantra.

It is obviously a misapplication of the term to speak of God as having a mantra in this sense, but God does have a mantra in the message he repeats over and over again to his children, hoping we will hear. We find it repeated for us time and again in the Sacred

Scriptures: I am with you. I love you. Trust me. It is hard to imagine any message that could be more comforting or consoling as a promise from our Creator and Father, who holds the whole world in his hands. God says to all of us and to each one of us personally: I am with you. I love you. Trust me.

God's promise to be with us began at the beginning—with Abraham, our father in faith, who was asked to set out on a perilous journey with no clear destination, but with the promise "I am your shield" (Gen 15:1). Saint Gregory of Nyssa's comment on Abraham's unquestioning response is classic: "Abraham left his home without knowing where he was going, a sure sign he was going the right way." When Abraham's son Isaac was doubtful, God reassured him: "You have no need to fear, since I am with you" (Gen 26:24). The same message was given to Jacob (28:15), Moses (Exod 3:12), Joshua (Josh 1:5), and to all the prophets and leaders of God's people. Jesus embodied this promise in the name Emmanuel (God is with us), and in his turn promised the same to his disciples: "And behold, I am with you always, until the end of the age" (Matt 28:20). I will be with you. I love you. Trust me.

Over and over again God told the people that he chose them out of love: "It was not because you are the largest of all nations that the LORD set his heart on you and chose you. . . . It was because the LORD loved you" (Deut 7:7-8). "[Y]ou are precious in my eyes and glorious. . . . / Fear not, for I am with you" (Isa 43:4-5). "With age-old love I have loved you; so I have kept my mercy toward you" (Jer 31:3). Jesus is the ultimate proof of that love: "God so loved the world that he gave his only Son" (John 3:16). "God is love. In this way the love of God was revealed to us: God sent his only Son into the world so that we might have life through him" (1 John 4:8-9). I am with you. I love you. Trust me.

When Jesus healed people he said, "Your faith has saved you" (Matt 9:22; Mark 5:34; 10:52; Luke 7:50; 8:48; 17:19; 18:42). He did not mean healing grace came to them because they understood everything about him, but it came because they put their trust in him as God's servant. They were open to God in him. They knew they could put their hope in him. "Your trust has saved you." We are not required to have vast information about Jesus, but we must seek to know him personally and commit our lives in trust to him. We can trust him, as we can trust his Father, to lead us on our pilgrim journey: "Commit your way to the LORD; / trust that God will act" (Ps 37:5). "Trust God at all times" (Ps 62:9). I am with you. I love you. Trust me.

In our daily life the path is often unclear. We don't know which way to turn, and we are tempted to believe that no one is in charge, nobody cares, and no one is listening. This darkness is the necessary context for the struggle of faith, so that we may freely choose for or against God. In the midst of this struggle it is most consoling to realize that God's main revelation to us about himself is that he loves us, watches over each of us at every moment, and desperately wants us to live with him forever. If this is not true, nothing is true. Behind all the trials and troubles of the world a constant message pulsates throughout the universe, like the rhythmic beating of God's heart: I am with you. I love you. Trust me.

The Silence of Mary

Images of Mary, the mother of Jesus, are found in collections of great art, religious and secular, around the world. The favorite subjects are the annunciation, the birth in Bethlehem, Mary at the cross, and the Madonna and Child (including the *Pietà*). These are frozen frames that give an impression of still life, but they pulsate with action. However, the action is within and is accessible to the viewer only from within.

The annunciation scene portrays the most momentous dialogue in history. The question is delivered and the response is awaited. The decisive action is within the heart of the maid, who is depicted in an attitude of wonder, openness, and pondering, and all time stands still. It is a moment of contemplation, in which the word of God is waiting for the response of the creature, like the finger of God reaching for Adam's hand in the Sistine Chapel. The word coming forever out of Mary's contemplation is *Fiat*, "Let it be done."

The scenes about Mary are all scenes about Jesus and her response to him. Her response is always captured in a silence that is filled with the one word, *Fiat*. Nothing else needs to be said and nothing else that would be said could improve on that response of this mother to this son, redeemed to redeemer. The scenes of silence pulsate with energy and deep communion.

Mary says very little in the gospels, certainly not as much as we would expect from the one through whom God set the work of redemption in motion, the one who is the mother of the Redeemer and is given to us as our mother. She listens to the angel, she responds, she lives the life laid out for her, she suffers, she observes, and she waits, "[keeping] all these things, reflecting on them in her heart" (Luke 2:19). She is very active, but her action, between herself and God, is unseen; it is in the heart, a contemplative action.

The silence of Mary is an essential ingredient of the life of the church. When it is lacking, no amount of fervor will cover up the nagging sense that something is missing. But we often respond to that feeling of emptiness by more words and more actions, even more prayerful words and more holy actions. But nothing will replace the silence of Mary.

Perhaps it is the increasing din of the modern world that is intensifying the present search for oases of silence. Retreat centers and hermitages are more and more popular, as are workshops and publications on prayer, especially quiet and contemplative prayer. This interest ranges far beyond the Catholic Church. In fact, many, if not most, of the contemporary books applying monastic values to lay life come from other Christians.

Or it may be that the life of worship within the Christian churches is not leaving enough room for the silence of Mary. Even many Catholics who appreciate the liturgical renewal of the Second Vatican Council miss the long silent periods of the Latin Mass. And many Protestants have begun to wonder whether in correcting abuses in medieval liturgy their ancestors did not discard an essential contemplative dimension that is still edged out in worship services of constant word and song, when even periods of private prayer are not silent. Our hearts yearn to rest wordlessly in the love of Jesus, like the silent Mary gazing at her newborn infant, or watching from afar at Nazareth, or holding his lifeless body, spent in love.

The resurgence of the rosary may be partly explained by this growing yearning for contemplative union. And not only among Catholics: there is an Anglican rosary now, though of different design and method, and a Lutheran way of using the rosary with a "biblical" Hail Mary, omitting the second part of the prayer. The beauty of the rosary has always been that it may be used in different ways, either with mental attention to the mysteries and even to the words of the prayer, or only as a bodily means of focusing our desire on God in quiet and contemplative union. And it may also be used whatever our situation or mood, when because of anguish, or sickness, or tiredness, or distraction we find it impossible to concentrate. Fingering the beads makes it possible for us to seek God at a different level, underneath the physical, mental, or emotional barricades.

The silence of Mary in the gospels is not an empty silence. It is a silence of waiting, of pondering, of loving. This contemplative silence is an essential ingredient of the life of the church and of each believer, and in our busy time we are hungering for it with new urgency. At first we are surprised by Mary's silence, and then, in the presence of Jesus, we understand.

Watch the Signs

God is constantly acting in our lives, but often that work is hidden under camouflage. As Cardinal Newman said, "His hand is ever over his own, and he leads them forward by a way they know not of." Only if we stay attentive and look closely will we get even a glimpse of the hand of God working in our lives. This is not by accident. The way to salvation is through faith, which means putting our trust in God. We could never grow in trust if the works of God's hand among us were visible and unmistakable.

Mostly we are given glimpses through signs that come and go in our lives day by day. If we are not looking for God's hand, we can easily miss the signs. We have to be paying attention. Usually we see the signs of God's activity in looking back; rarely can we be confident about exactly what God is doing in the present.

Some years ago I went to Pine Bluff, about 130 miles from the abbey in southeast Arkansas, for the burial of my good friend Frank King, who had died suddenly a few days before. My whole attention was on Frank and his friendship, and on the family and friends with whom I would share some time. I didn't know there was more to my trip than that. I didn't know until later that God was using Frank to put me in place to be available to act as an instrument in God's plan for a third party. Frank had been a deacon, and we had often ministered together. I was going to mourn Frank, but that was only the part of the picture I could see. He and I were going to team up for an act of ministry again.

The bishop had recently requested prayers for sick clergy and because of this I knew that one of the priests in the diocese was in intensive care at the hospital in Pine Bluff, very ill and even in danger of death. This was Father Bernard Keller, SVD, a wonderful priest and friend, pastor of St. Peter's Church in Pine Bluff. I looked up the address of the hospital and planned to visit Father Bernie after Frank's funeral.

The funeral Mass for Frank was held in Little Rock in the morning, and the burial was at Pine Bluff in the afternoon. After the service I made my way to the hospital and asked at the front desk for directions to ICU. "I guess you're here to see Father Keller," the receptionist said. "He's very low."

When I reached the ICU hallway and visiting area, several people turned and smiled, and some whom I recognized came toward me. "It's so good that you have come. We didn't expect anyone to come all that way. Father is in a coma but the family will be so glad you made it." I soon understood that Father Bernie had been asking for a priest before he slipped into a coma, but the other Catholic pastor was out of town. He seemed to be hanging on until he could receive a blessing from a priest. The people had been calling around other towns to find a priest and praying that one would come. They thought I had heard about it and had come because of that search. I had not heard about the search but had come, without knowing it, in answer to their prayers.

I went in to see Father Bernie who was indeed in his final struggle. The nurse told me there wasn't much keeping him alive, and they thought he would have died before this. I blessed him and prayed with the family for a while. Then I went back to the waiting room to visit with his parishioners and friends. Several came toward me for a report. I had barely begun talking with them when the ICU nurse, who had come up behind me, touched my elbow and said, "Father, he's gone."

It broke upon me then that I had known only part of the reason I was going to Pine Bluff that day. I thought I had been in charge of my trip, but I was moving according to another plan. I felt very blessed and humbled to have been an instrument in God's hands, though ignorant of what was going on until the moment it happened, to be the one chosen to help a holy priest pass from this life to eternity surrounded by those who loved him. I realized that Frank King had been as much a part of it as I, and that this was a special gift for both of us to be able to minister together one last time. It was a special reminder to me of how close God is all the time, taking care of us and walking with us even when we're not conscious of that guiding presence.

Sabbath

A few years ago a Presbyterian pastor wrote an article for *Christianity Today* titled "Confessions of a Former Sabbath Breaker." He said that though "keeping the Sabbath" is one of the Ten Commandments, he found that, far from being reprimanded by the church when he broke that commandment, he was rewarded. He was not able to keep a Sabbath on Sunday, which is a workday for a pastor, but neither did he observe the Sabbath on any other day of the week. He kept up a frantic pace all week, and for this was compensated with "the largest single annual increase in salary I have ever received."

The Sabbath is a gift of God that came to the world through the Hebrews. The name means "rest," but another word, "holy," is also connected with the day; from early Israelite times the Sabbath was a holy day marked by religious observance. No one knows how the Sabbath originated, though later generations connected it with the creation and with liberation from slave work in Egypt. After the Babylonian exile, the Sabbath became a hallmark of true religious observance for Jews.

The Sabbath is ultimately an act of faith in the loving providence of God. I can lay down my tools and cease my constant striving for one day a week and the world will not fall apart, my life will not fall apart. Today the religious Sabbath is under heavy attack. Differences between one day and another are systematically obliterated. Commercially, Sunday is becoming like every other day. But the process reaches further than that: in some places there is hardly any difference even between night and day. We cannot pause to rest. And what is it that we cannot rest from? Under whatever disguise our striving hides, inability to rest comes from a relentless search for security, which, in a person of biblical faith, is a lack of trust in God.

On the other hand, it is precisely at this time that the busy world is discovering the need for Sabbath in every life. Everywhere there are stress seminars and exercise programs, teaching people to rest, pause, slow down, smell the roses. The world and my life will not fall apart if I pause, but they will fall apart if I don't; that is the message coming around now from the secular side. We are catching up with biblical wisdom, though for the wrong reasons. The Sabbath is not mainly for good health, but for good life: a good trusting relationship with a good God. The present Sabbath rest is a foreshadowing of the heavenly rest (Heb 4:9-11); learning to observe the Sabbath is a preparation for eternal life with God.

I have come to regard the revelation of the Sabbath as further evidence, stronger than many other "proofs," that God indeed broke into human history to save us and teach us how to live. The Sabbath came out of nowhere, with no preparation, answering a fundamental human need and providing a simple but powerful way to express regularly the meaning of our life with a loving God.

But the Sabbath is more than a "day off": it is a spiritual principle (and it just so happens, a life principle). We need a Sabbath day, but we also need the Sabbath in every day, a time when we trust enough to put the world on automatic pilot (God) and rest. This at its best we call prayer.

Saint Benedict did not mention Sabbath by name in writing his Rule, but he was a man so steeped in the Scriptures that the Sabbath principle pervades the life he set forth. This is highlighted especially by his provision for the "Work of God" (the Divine Office), which is like a Sabbath carved in slices out of the monk's day. As innocent as missing an hour of the Office may seem, St. Benedict insisted that "nothing is to be preferred to the Work of God" (43.3) and made eagerness for the Work of God one of the criteria for evaluating a novice (58.7). This exercise is a constant barometer of the monk's faith, because practically anything else can seem more important than prayer when the bell rings. And if I won't pray when the bell rings, why would I pray when it doesn't? Only by faith can we take a Sabbath rest time after time, letting God run his world without us.

Passion for control of our lives and of the world makes the Sabbath seem like a threat or, from another point of view, a luxury; but it is one of God's unsung gifts, a vital treasure. We can stumble over it every week or even every day and go racing on to get out of the territory or, like the man in the parable, recognize the treasure and buy the field (Matt 13:44).

Truth Is Beauty

Words from John Keats's *Ode on a Grecian Urn* have become immortal: "Beauty is truth, truth beauty,—that is all / Ye know on earth, and all ye need to know." How simple this seems, and perhaps at first sight, how obvious. Yet, it is not self-evident; otherwise we would all be absorbed in a relentless pursuit of the truth.

And we are not. Lying and deceiving have become commonsense approaches to getting ahead. Perjury, which used to be ranked with armed robbery, is now simply considered a white lie.

Perhaps in the decline of truth, we will recognize the beauty we have lost. Maybe the results of dishonesty and hypocrisy will convince us in a new way that "Beauty is truth, truth beauty." We have seen sad spectacles like the demise of Enron, where company leaders brought themselves and the company down by cheating and lying, and in their fall caused thousands of honest workers to lose their jobs and future retirements.

Jesus identified himself as "the way and the truth and the life" (John 14:6) and, hauled before the Roman authority, explained his cause as a mission of truth: "For this I was born and for this I came into the world, to testify to the truth. Everyone who belongs to the truth listens to my voice" (John 18:37). But Pilate responded as many in places of public trust have responded after him: "What is truth?" implying that the truth is what I make it; it is adjusted to current need by my "spin."

God has many names in the Hebrew Scriptures—Yahweh, El Shaddai, Adonai, Elohim—but God's identity is best revealed by the covenant virtues of love and truth, which constantly appear in tandem in many variations: "Praise the LORD, all you nations! / . . . The LORD's love for us is strong; / the LORD is faithful forever" (Ps 117:1-2). "[G]ood indeed is the LORD, / Whose love endures forever, / whose faithfulness lasts through every age" (Ps 100:5). Depending on the emphasis, this combination identifies God as faithful love or loving faithfulness.

That God is truth doesn't mean only that God tells the truth. God is faithful, firm, reliable, trustworthy, one you can hang on to and depend on. Among the many images for God in the psalms— shepherd, king, shield, light, eagle—by far the most common is rock. God is "my rock of refuge, . . . my stronghold" (Ps 18:3), "the rock of my heart" (Ps 73:26), "the rock of our salvation" (Ps 95:1). A rock is something strong, solid, dependable, something you can cling to and rely on when everything else is shaky.

Those familiar with the biblical tradition would have recognized what was being asserted about Jesus when the prologue of John's gospel described him as being "full of grace and truth" (John 1:14). These are the defining qualities of the God of revelation.

To be full of grace and truth, to be faithful in our love and loving in our fidelity, is the vocation of all disciples in the biblical tradition. The Letter to the Ephesians describes this in a beautiful phrase as "living the truth in love" (Eph 4:15) or, as it is literally in the Greek, "truthing in love." This is not just telling the truth, but being the truth, as God is.

We must not let go of this value, no matter how the truth may be mistreated, skirted, or manipulated. Truth is still beauty, and there is no way around the truth to the goals of a nation or society. Deceit destroys, but the truth sets free.

Caught between Accepting and Choosing

Some of God's prophets were not eager to be chosen. Jeremiah protested that he wasn't equipped for the job: "I know not how to speak; I am too young" (Jer 1:6). Gideon thought there must have been a mistake: "I am the most insignificant in my father's house" (Judg 6:15). But the most reluctant was Moses—or at least the Bible has a better record of his reluctance.

When God in the burning bush tells Moses he has come to rescue the Israelites from Egypt, Moses is all ears. This is what everyone has been waiting for. But then God goes on: "Come now! I will send you to Pharaoh to lead my people, the Israelites, out of Egypt" (Exod 3:10). Then Moses begins to backpedal. "Who am I that I should go to Pharaoh and lead the Israelites out of Egypt?" (Exod 3:11). In a series of five exchanges, Moses racks his brain to come up with some excuse that will convince God to change his mind. But God has made his choice and is not going to change.

Moses then accepts in obedience and performs well in launching the great effort of leading the vast people out of slavery: through the difficult negotiations with Pharaoh and the series of plagues, the flight from the Egyptian army to the sea, the miraculous crossing, and the first difficult days marching in the wilderness. But we still remember Moses' reluctance and might wonder whether he is wholeheartedly given to the project.

Then comes the scene with his father-in-law Jethro, who visits Moses in the wilderness, bringing along Moses' wife and children (Exod 18:1-12). After accepting some sage advice from Jethro, Moses bids farewell to his father-in-law, who then returns alone to Midian. Moses takes his family and sets out to lead the people to the Promised Land.

There is here a symbolic separation from the past. Moses is no longer holding on to the hope that his unwanted vocation will go away, and he embraces the call he had halfheartedly accepted at first. He assumes the role of leader totally and casts his lot with the people, so much so that later he says if the Lord will not forgive the sin of the people, he himself is willing to be stricken from the book (Exod 32:32).

In every vocation, whether it is a major life step or just an appointment or assignment along the way, there are these two steps of accepting the call and then choosing it. In the best circumstances, these steps happen simultaneously, but if the call is not appealing we may, like Moses, be able to make only one at a time. There is nothing wrong with trying for a better deal until the decision is final. Jesus asked his Father to take the cup away, but when it was clearly his vocation he embraced it: "[N]ot what I will but what you will" (Mark 14:36). The tragedy comes when we make the first step, accepting the call, but not the second, thus failing to embrace it and own it. Then we drag our call along, doing the work but in a joyless way and perhaps spreading bitterness as we go. We think it is the job that burdens us, but it is our attitude. We also think nobody knows, but we are exposed for all to see.

A parishioner may be elected chairman of the parish council and accept the job as a necessary evil but serve with dragging feet, not only wasting the opportunity but draining the morale of other members. A priest may accept the assignment to a new parish, but make it obvious that the change was not his idea. A religious may accept an appointment in obedience but hold on to the hope that it will go away, treading water in the meantime. The danger of getting caught between the acceptance and the embrace of a calling can happen in the smallest things—doing the dishes or carrying out the trash—as well as in the monumental things: embracing an irreversible life situation, such as a terminal illness or the birth of a child with Down syndrome. These assignments and conditions will not be life-giving until they are chosen and the person called rises above personal desires and ambitions to embrace them as the call of God.

Moses had good reasons to question God's choice and try to back out: he had already had two full careers and by biblical reckoning was eighty years old, there might still have been a price on his head in Egypt, and by this time he was an outsider to the enslaved community. But God insisted, and Moses accepted. At first he could do no more than perform his responsibilities with an eye cast fondly back to his pre–burning bush days. But at a graced moment he embraced the call of God. This gave him inner freedom and he never looked back again.

I Am Invisible

I am invisible. Or almost. I am becoming invisible. I need your help before I disappear completely. You think you see me but you don't.

When people look at me they often don't see me in my primary identity in the church (after baptism). What they see is a Catholic priest. And that's true enough. I am a priest and very happy to be identified as one. But that's my second layer. My first layer is invisible.

My first and primary layer is as a member of a religious order in the church. It's not the same thing as priesthood. My first identity is as a religious, a Benedictine monk. I was a monk before I was a priest, and I became a priest as part of my monastic obedience. But most people see me primarily as a priest.

Is that bad? No, and if it were happening only to me, it wouldn't be worth mentioning. But it is happening to male religious in general. Thousands of us are becoming invisible, and what we represent is in danger of disappearing from public consciousness. Whenever one of the many and varied expressions of Catholic life becomes invisible, it is a diminishment in the rich tapestry that is life in the Catholic Church.

For some of us this is nothing new. The most invisible group in religious life in the church are the religious brothers. Every parish has the ministry of a priest, but the presence of a brother is rare, depending on whether brothers are involved in a special ministry in the parish, such as education or spiritual formation. Some brothers are well known locally in monasteries and in ministries of education, health care, and service of the poor. But often, when a brother shows up, people don't know how to take him. Why don't you go all the way? Or, why aren't you a priest? Did you flunk out?

The awareness of men's religious life is fading out of the everyday consciousness of the Catholic faithful. Sometimes it even drops off the screen of bishops and parish priests. A typical reference in calls for church vocations is for "priests and sisters." Even when the usage is "priests and religious" it usually means the same thing, because what flashes through our minds is a group of men who are priests and a group of women who are religious. Several years ago a new ministry was being promoted in our diocese. In order to handle the number of those who had to be trained, one day was scheduled for informing the priests, another for the religious. I signed up for the one for religious, assuming that the session for priests was primarily for pastors of parishes. All the participants of the day for religious were sisters, except for two male Carmelites and me. A lay volunteer helping to arrange the meetings asked me, "What are you doing here? This is for religious."

Part of it is my own fault. When I appear in public I don't ordinarily wear my monastic habit but a clerical shirt or suit, which is the identifying garb of a priest. I have to admit I am contributing to the problem by doing this. But even if I wore the monastic habit everywhere I went, it would be one small drop in a very large ocean, especially in states like Arkansas, where there are very few male religious. Anyway, monks are in the minority among men religious who now regularly wear a religious habit even in their home communities.

Why is this invisibility troubling me? I have already mentioned the diminishment to the rich tapestry of life in the Catholic Church. There is another reason, too, of more immediate concern. Everyone speaks of a vocation crisis in the church, meaning there aren't as many priests and religious as there were before, not enough to meet what we perceive as the need, and the number is declining. One sure way to make that crisis worse is to carry on with a diminishing awareness of men's religious life in the church. Of the younger (and older) men in our society with a religious vocation, some are called to be diocesan priests, others are called to be ordained religious, and others are called to be religious without ordination. Men called to the religious life do not necessarily have a priestly vocation. And even for those who do, a major difference between the call to the diocesan priesthood and the call to priesthood within the religious life is that an essential aspect of the latter is living one's vocation in community with other vowed men.

When a Catholic man feels God tugging at his heart and seeks guidance and help from other members of the church, if all we think is available for a man with such a calling in the church is a vocation to the diocesan priesthood, we will assist him toward the diocesan seminary. Well and good when that is his vocation. But he may be called to serve God in a religious community, and instead of assisting him, we may confuse and possibly discourage him because we don't have the full Catholic vocation context in our own awareness. He may be called to be a brother, or to be a diocesan priest, or to be a religious priest, and for a while he may not know which it is. God will depend on us to help him find out. A one-size-fits-all approach could lose religious vocations for the church.

Celibacy

A sociological survey several years ago found that 62 percent of diocesan priests would marry if the law of mandatory celibacy were relaxed. At that time Father Joseph Fichter, SJ, a noted sociologist, remarked that when he went into an airport wearing his collar, people wondered whether he was among the 62 percent of frustrated priests or the 38 percent of weirdos.

In all the debates on the issue of celibacy, I find an important ingredient missing. The arena is always "the mandatory celibacy of the clergy." That's fair enough, but I bet because of all the media folderol most people don't realize that the large majority of those who have made a public commitment of celibacy in the church are not in the clergy category. Most of us are "religious" (members of religious orders), and our celibacy has nothing to do with priesthood. Therefore, the question of the mandatory celibacy of the clergy (an important question, granted) doesn't affect us personally any more than it would our parents. The point is this: we didn't become celibates because it was a requirement for a ministry we felt called to; it was because celibacy was an integral part of a life to which we felt called. That part of the life won't change: we don't expect it to, and we don't want it to.

But don't get me wrong. The number of religious (or priests) who pursue celibacy as a goal in itself is probably pretty small. It wasn't a goal for me. I didn't wake up as a teenager one morning and say to myself: "Gee, I think I'll be a celibate. That sounds like fun!" What I was interested in and felt God calling me to was a way of life, a life close to God and dedicated to serving him and helping his people. I encountered some fascinating, talented, dedicated, happy people in the religious life serving as teachers, nurses, farmers, pastors, coaches—and I felt the Lord tugging at my heart. That was the life God was weaving for me, and celibacy was part of it. And so I went for that life.

"Why didn't you want to get married?" Well, I did want to get married, but I wanted something else more, something I felt God was calling me to. Being chosen for something and choosing came together. "In all your years of celibacy, haven't you met someone you would really like to share your life with, to be married to, some woman who would make your life wonderful?" Yes, I have to admit it, I have; and it's more than one: I haven't been keeping track, but by now it must be about four thousand. It isn't because I don't like women or marriage that I'm a celibate.

"Then why is it?" I'm only beginning to realize. Somehow it's because in a way different from most people—a way I'll probably never completely understand—over the years Jesus' love, like a bomb blast in slow motion, has blown my heart into a million pieces, and I'll never be able to put it back together and give it to anyone but to God.

"But do you really think, with all these statistics against you, that you'll be able to remain faithful to your celibacy?" Yes, I do, mainly because the one who has called me is faithful; and there are ways to cooperate with his faithful care. First of all, I try not to lie to myself. I don't tell myself that celibacy comes naturally and that I can live any old way I please and still remain faithful. My hormones didn't make vows. I know that I can't read just anything or watch just anything the entertainment media offers. I can't sneak a peek at internet porn and eagerly listen to suggestive jokes and expect to stay spiritually healthy and at peace. I know that I must instead renew my mind constantly with readings dipped from the pure deep well of Scripture and tradition. I cannot permit a society that doesn't understand my values to set my norms. And

I know that I need self-denial, less popular today than ever. But as *Poor Richard's Almanac* puts it: "A fat kitchen makes a lean will." Even without the negative press I know that what I am trying to do is against the odds. I am too weak for this. So I look elsewhere for the strength to pull it off. I look to my brothers in community, who help me by their faithfulness, their example, their love. I get support from my family and from other men and women who care for me and share my values. But this only works if I am in touch with the One who called me. God reaches me with my brothers in our daily Divine Office, our Mass, and the sacraments. More than anything, I depend on daily silent communion with the Lord, opening myself in all my vulnerability to Jesus Christ, to whom I don't have to explain anything, because he was where I am long before me. Private prayer is where I become a celibate again every day.

I might be able to remain technically faithful from now on without prayer, just from the pride of being a hardheaded German who would hate to cash it all in after qualifying for AARP. But celibacy is not just a matter of gritting your teeth: ideally it makes one free, joyful, loving, available for many people without using or binding anyone. Without prayer, I might be sexually reproachless, but become an icicle, snarling when someone takes the funnies ahead of me, or depressed for days because of the way my handkerchiefs are folded.

As it is, I am full of hope about celibacy, in my own life and in the life of the church. I'm even hopeful about marriage, which may make me a real visionary.

Christian Life:
With and In Community

The God of Hearsay

One of the most chilling aftermaths to the terrorist attacks of September 11, 2001, came to me not from newspapers or TV but from the pages of a biblical review. *The Biblical Theology Bulletin*, in an editorial titled "Religion's Bitter Fruits," reported on a television interview of the daughter of a famous American evangelical preacher. The interviewer, a Jew, asked her whether Jews can be saved. The interviewee compared God to her father, who lives in a gated community and can be reached only by invitation. Those not invited are not welcome. God has the right to set limits, she said, and he has not invited those who are not born again in Jesus. The kingdom of God is a gated community.

Many of the great atrocities of history, including the September 11 attacks, have their origins in a rigid religious orthodoxy. This type of orthodoxy leads to intolerance and persecution, which is not simply a thing of the past. There were more martyrs of religion worldwide in the year 2000 than in any year of the previous millennium. We have noticed in the present world conflicts the tendency on both sides to characterize opponents as evil and to trace their problem to a misguided idea of God, with the implication that we ourselves are good and our idea of God is correct. From the American side there was also the early reaction to September 11 that terrorists hate us because we are good, an assumption that is its own commentary.

The Bible is harsh and unyielding in its prohibition of idolatry, the worship of something that is not God. In the Old Testament, this takes the form of prohibition of images to represent God, a practice that had caused Israel's neighbors to confuse the image with the reality. There is nothing in the New Testament prohibiting images; the danger has been removed because we have the true image or icon of God in Jesus (Col 1:15). But the prohibition of idols remains (1 John 5:21), though now the emphasis has moved inside, to the heart, where we might be bowing down to a god like avarice (Eph 5:5) or gluttony (Phil 3:19).

The Bible's most penetrating teaching on idolatry is not in the prohibition of stone idols but in the story of Job. Job was a good man, described even by God as "blameless and upright, fearing God and avoiding evil" (Job 1:8). But Job was genuinely mistaken about God. He thought God was simply a scorekeeper who rewards the good with prosperity and punishes the wicked with suffering. Until he was tested by a series of personal tragedies, Job's experience supported this notion of God. He was good and he was rich. But his suffering put his experience in direct challenge to his theology. Why was he suffering? What right had God to punish him? He held on in faith without understanding—to his everlasting credit—but he poured out his soul in self-righteous anger because God was not behaving as expected.

God remained silent during the long monologues of Job and his friends, but finally God spoke, and from that divine intervention Job received a stunning and saving insight. He realized that he had been out of his depth: "I have dealt with great things that I do not understand; / things too wonderful for me, which I cannot know." He found that his concept of God was an illusion; he had not known who God was until then: "I knew you only by hearsay, but now I have seen you with my own eyes" (42:3, 5).

Everyone begins knowing God by hearsay: initially from parents, and eventually from teachers, pastors, friends, the media. Some of these people know God personally and truly, but others only know by hearsay themselves, and they pass on to us the true or the false, the good or the bad in their understanding. Is it any wonder that the God we know by hearsay shares the priorities and preferences of our sources? To become truly children of God, we must meet the true God on our own or we may still be clutching an idol in sight of the Promised Land.

The story of Job tells us we can be "blameless and upright" and still wrong about God. The self-deception can go so far as to be a kind of idolatry. It is especially dangerous when things are going our way. We find that our God has the same values and attitudes, and even prejudices, as ourselves. When we pray, we use a lot of words to remind God what these are, but we are loath to listen to God, who might differ with us.

The present international crises have significant religious components. They may even be described on a certain level as a conflict of idolatries: false images of God driving us further and further apart. The more that all of us strive to know God personally, and not only by hearsay, the greater the likelihood of our discovering God's kingdom is not a gated community to which we have exclusive access—and the greater the possibility of our understanding one another and reconciling our differences.

Coldhearted Orthodoxy

Ephesus had a premier reputation among the Christian communities of the early church. Tradition linked it with Mary the Mother of Jesus and the apostle John. Paul made it the hub of his evangelizing ministry for two years. An influential Pauline letter was addressed to the Ephesian congregation.

It is no wonder that the book of Revelation, written late in the first century, gives Ephesus pride of place in the letters of Jesus to the seven churches of Asia Minor. Jesus speaks words of commendation to this renowned congregation: "I know your works, your labor, and your endurance, and that you cannot tolerate the wicked; you have tested those who call themselves apostles but are not, and discovered that they are impostors" (Rev 2:2). Ephesus has proved itself worthy of the trust shown it by the great apostles.

This faithfulness has not been easy: "Moreover, you have endurance and have suffered for my name, and you have not grown weary" (v. 3). The Christians in Ephesus have paid a price for remaining vigilant and for remaining firm under relentless attack from a hostile society. They have taken their place of leadership seriously, preserving the orthodox teaching in spite of persecution.

Their achievement is highlighted in contrast to the failures of two other communities. Pergamum tolerates in its midst "some people there who hold to the teaching of Balaam . . . [and] some who hold to the teaching of [the] Nicolaitans" (vv. 14, 15). Thyatira tolerates a "Jezebel" who "teaches and misleads my servants to play the harlot and to eat food sacrificed to idols" (v. 20). The groups alluded to here advocated in various ways a compromise with the pagan environment involving a softening of morals and religious boundaries and a blurring of orthodox teaching. These tendencies have not been allowed to gain a foothold in Ephesus.

Labor, endurance, standing up for the truth, suffering for the name of Jesus, and not growing weary—any Christian would rejoice to hear these words of praise from Jesus. But Jesus is not finished. He recognizes the good in Ephesus, but he also has a serious criticism: "Yet I hold this against you: you have lost the love you had at first" (v. 4).

Lost the love! That stings to the heart. Ephesus is the community of John the Beloved, whose whole teaching may be summarized as a summons to love: "God is love, and whoever remains in love remains in God and God in him" (1 John 4:16). Jesus makes clear how serious is the charge and the failing: "Realize how far you have fallen. . . . Otherwise, I will come to you and remove your lampstand from its place, unless you repent" (Rev 2:5). Removal of the lampstand would mean deposing Ephesus from its exalted position among the churches: it could be leader no more.

How has Ephesus failed? How has it fallen? The irony is that its failure has the same source as its excellence: the community's dedication to orthodox teaching. In championing true Christian teaching, the leaders of the church of Ephesus have gradually become watchdogs instead of shepherds, quick to condemn and cast out: "[Y]ou cannot tolerate the wicked" (v. 2). The community prides itself on orthodoxy but has become harsh and unloving toward the erring and misguided. It has forgotten patience, gentleness, and compassion in its concern for orthodoxy, and it needs to listen again to the original gospel message underlying the cherished formulas: "For this is the message you have heard from the beginning: we should love one another" (1 John 3:11).

We live today in a situation that has much in common with the Ephesus of AD 95. Society is hostile to our values and wants us to modify our faith convictions and lower our moral standards. There are those among us who, in their desire to preserve Catholic orthodoxy, can become heavy-handed and coldhearted. An article on the status of a major American diocese commented on a subgroup that sees itself as the orthodox Catholics with a mission to force the rest into line, in effect, trying to hold the local church hostage to their views.

We must not repeat the error of Ephesus, a good community with a strong Christian tradition, which in pursuing error fell into the most serious error of all: failure to love. Orthodoxy and love are both important, but love is the Great Commandment. No one has said it better than Paul, a champion of orthodoxy himself, writing in Ephesus forty years before the crisis described above: "[I]f I have the gift of prophecy, and comprehend all mysteries and all knowledge; if I have all faith so as to move mountains but do not have love, I am nothing" (1 Cor 13:2).

The Covenant of Salt

Twice the Hebrew Bible uses the puzzling expression, "covenant of salt." Speaking to Aaron, God said: "All the holy offerings that the Israelites present to the LORD I have given to you, together with your sons and daughters, as a perpetual due; it is a covenant of salt forever before the LORD for you and your descendants as well" (Num 18:19, NRSV).

A few hundred years later Abijah, king of Judah, spoke to his opponents of the northern kingdom as they prepared for war: "Do you not know that the LORD, the God of Israel, has given the Kingdom of Israel to David forever, to him and to his sons, by a covenant made in salt?" (2 Chr 13:5).

We are familiar with the use of "covenant" to describe the promise of salvation by which God bound himself to Israel, a pact brought to completion in the "new covenant" in the blood of Jesus. But why the salt?

In the ancient world sharing a meal with someone was a sacred occasion that formed a special relationship. People did not easily invite strangers from other clans to their common meal. A shared meal created a bond, a covenant, which guaranteed nonaggression and even defense of one another in time of trouble. To break the bond created by the meal was a serious social crime. We find echoes of this in Psalm 41:10, which Jesus quoted of Judas at the Last Supper: "But so that the scripture might be fulfilled, 'The one who ate my food has raised his heel against me'" (John 13:18).

Salt was regarded as a necessary ingredient of the daily menu (before the days of high blood pressure). Thus it was easy and natural to connect salt with the family or friendship relationship expressed by a shared meal. An Arabic expression among friends, used from time immemorial, is "There is salt between us." The use of salt in Israel's ritual sacrifices stressed the intimate relationship of God with his people.

Though we do not use the expression "covenant of salt," the reality it signifies is present even in our fast-food society. Most families still have special meals that express family unity; prime examples are Thanksgiving and Christmas meals and, more rarely now, Sunday dinner.

In monasteries, the principal community meal of the day is a primary event in the religious observance. It is designed as a reflection and even continuation of the Eucharist, a further sharing at the table of the covenant renewed around the altar. In his Rule, St. Benedict treats table service as a sacred ministry, entered upon and concluded with blessing ceremonies. This sets a tone of care and reverence within which the bread and wine of his typical meal, along with the reading of Scripture, emphasize the connections between Eucharist and community meal.

Besides giving flavor, salt is also a preservative. This quality lends itself well to expressing the enduring nature of a covenant: note the phrase "forever" in the biblical passages quoted earlier. The family meal is a natural ritual that binds us to one another, so it served as the ideal model for the covenant meal of the Eucharist. Both the family meal and the Eucharist are "covenants of salt," sealing and strengthening the sacred bonds that unite us with one another. This awareness makes a saying of Jesus in the Gospel of Mark all the more suggestive: "Keep salt in yourselves and you will have peace with one another" (9:50).

Prosperity Theology

Except for the first centuries of the church, there has not been much creativity in the making of Christian heresies. Usually a new erroneous teaching is a repetition or varia-tion of a heresy from earlier days. Most heresies revolve around the triune God, the divine and human natures of Jesus, the nature of the church, and the action of grace in the life of the believer.

Heresy is a serious issue, but most heretics are innocent. By that I mean that in the church's division of heresy into formal (pur-posely holding falsehood) and material (accidentally holding false-hood), rarely is anyone in the first category. To be a formal heretic, you have to be guilty of "obstinate post-baptismal denial" of a truth of the faith (*Catechism of the Catholic Church*, 2089). That is very rare. Most of our errors are a matter of not paying attention.

When we have a hard time seeing how Jesus could make some of the same mistakes growing up that we made, for example, we don't mean to deny that he is fully human.

It may be that such a rarity—a new Christian heresy—is present in a teaching that is gaining ground today. In this case, economic conditions had to be just right for it to happen. I refer to what is being called the "prosperity gospel" or "prosperity theology," a teaching that the way to be financially well-off is to be good. It is even broader than that, proposing that a faithful Christian will be healthy as well as wealthy.

You might expect such a teaching to be dismissed with a laugh, since everyone can see there is no correlation between being good and being rich and healthy. Some of the holiest people in the world are poor, and some of the most evil are rich. Cancer wards are filled with both the good and the bad. Only in the affluent West could the prosperity gospel have a hearing. Try to preach it to faithful Christians in Darfur or Iraq.

More amazing is how a doctrine that goes directly against the teaching of Jesus can be called Christian. Jesus says anyone who wants to be his follower must deny himself and take up the cross (Mark 8:34). He says, "[W]oe to you who are rich" (Luke 6:24), and that it is easier for a camel to pass through the eye of a needle than for a rich person to enter the kingdom (Matt 19:24). He tells the rich young man to sell what he has and give it to the poor; "[T]hen come, follow me" (Mark 10:21).

Prosperity theology can be persuasive because its proponents avoid this stream of texts and concentrate on other texts that are more ambiguous. A favorite passage is "I came so that they might have life and have it more abundantly" (John 10:10). Jesus' words are taken to mean that the abundant life he wants for us is to be well-off in this world, but everything in the context of John's gospel and the New Testament tells us that this is precisely what he doesn't promise us. "Abundant life" is not a gift of this world; it is far beyond anything this world has to offer.

That being said, there is nothing wrong with being wealthy. It is the love of money, not money itself, that is "the root of all evils" (1 Tim 6:10). We should be thankful for riches and use them responsibly and wisely in service of God and one another. But Jesus himself said riches are dangerous (whatever they are: money, property, good health, intellectual ability, athletic ability) since they can deceive us into thinking we are independent and in control of our own lives. Then they deprive us of abundant life.

Most heretics are innocent, but the error they teach can be very harmful, both to themselves and to the people who assimilate their teaching. When a dedicated moral and spiritual life is not rewarded with worldly riches and earthly happiness—as this teaching promises it should—or when, instead, disaster strikes, the result may be disillusionment and a sense of divine betrayal. It can lead even to a rejection of the Christian faith. Meanwhile, the real promise is lost: the spiritual abundance we might receive by binding our sufferings to the cross.

Jesus did not promise that we would have worldly riches, nor did he promise that we wouldn't. He did promise that those who follow him faithfully will have eternal life, and he told us that to follow him faithfully we must take up the cross.

The Christian Reflex

One of the most influential books on American democracy was written by a Frenchman who visited here for less than a year in 1831 and 1832. Alexis de Tocqueville, like many Frenchmen still reeling from the chaotic effects of the French Revolution, was trying to envision the society of the future. He came to examine the American experience of democracy; his razor-sharp analysis still stands up in many aspects to this day. Rare is the week that his name is not invoked somewhere in political or social commentary.

In recent years, Tocqueville's warnings about the danger of excessive individualism in democracy have received new attention. He was concerned that pursuit of equality, initially designed to promote the good of all and not just certain classes, might veer off into a pursuit of selfishness. Citizens would create their own islands in the society, viewing other individuals or groups with suspicion or hostility, rather than trying to create a common life for the common good. At best, a person would then withdraw into a circle of family and friends, where, safely ensconced, he "gladly leaves the greater society to look after itself."

Some would say that Tocqueville's fears in that regard are being realized. Many examples are given: the rape of the environment for personal gain without regard to people downstream, either geographically or historically; exorbitant CEO incomes while employees are struggling; exploitation of the Medicare system.

Democracy is not to blame for these excesses, which are the effects of sin in the world. Tocqueville's point was that democratic "equality" (which he regarded as the way of the future) needed a strong common moral vision to keep it from disaster. Otherwise there would be no reason for self-restraint; democracy would then lead instead to more inequality, and the system would have to be held together by more laws and more prisons.

What gave him hope at the time was the common moral consensus that he perceived in America, based on the convictions of a widely shared Christianity. Today that consensus has been badly shaken, and the present moral vacuum may be the seedbed for the very problems that Tocqueville dreaded.

But what if authentic Christian principles would reclaim their place in the society? What does Christianity have to offer to the moral climate to protect "equality" from ending up in selfish individualism?

The Christian reflex is optimism, trust, and hope. Unredeemed, we face the world with fear. Our reflex is suspicion, self-protection, condemnation. This is destructive to any society building, not to say any human communication. We require each person and situation to prove itself, explain itself, defend itself before we let our guard down. But faith opens our eyes to a world blessed by God's presence.

When meeting a new person or a new situation, the Christian looks first for the good, the opportunity, the blessing. Circumstances may require the second movement almost immediately to be one of caution and judgment, because we must be shrewd as serpents as well as innocent as doves. But that is at least a split-second later. Trust and hope come first. A statement of Goethe shows how powerfully this approach works in personal relationships (and for the common good): "Treat people as if they were what they ought to be and you help them become what they are capable of being."

The opposite of this open attitude of trust and hope is the mind-set revealed in the rallying cry "safe sex," which may come to stand as a symbol for our generation. To offer oneself to the other defensively in this most sacred human act is the ultimate distortion of human relations. The sexual act among humans is not the instinctive reflex of animals but a decision to open oneself in complete vulnerability to the other because of the trust that exists by the commitment of love. It is meant to be a pattern to strive for in all other human communication. For achievement of growth into personhood and for the destiny of the human race, "safe sex" is the most unsafe sex of all.

The Christian reflex is also community. There is no such thing as a solo Christian. Community life is a consequence of New Testament faith. This is brought home with special force in the Acts of the Apostles, where Saul, even after his dramatic conversion, had to accept membership in the community by baptism, and where it was by joining the group of believers that one was added to the Lord (see Acts 5:14). In the community, the disciple of Jesus learned to live for others as the Master did; the Christian reflex is not individualistic nor selfish but loving: "Do not seek your own advantage, but that of the other" (1 Cor 10:24, NRSV).

Tocqueville had high hopes for America's ability to make democratic equality a source of liberty and justice for all, especially because of what he perceived as the nation's adoption of the Christian view that "we must do good to our fellows for love of God." That vision is under threat today because of the inroads of extreme individualism, and it may be up to Christians more than ever before to keep it alive by bringing to bear the hopeful, loving, unselfish life made possible by the grace of Christ.

Over-responsibility

Everyone likes to be known as a responsible person. It's a compliment to be described as having a "sense of responsibility." We know how valuable a responsible member— one you can always count on—is to any group. Words like "accountability," "commitment," "faithfulness" have a positive ring.

Many of the woes of society are attributed to a failure of responsibility: "Mistakes were made." "The department I was in charge of had errors in bookwork." Adam blamed Eve; Eve blamed the snake. When Washington DC drew criticism for its high crime rate, Mayor Marion Berry defended his administration by saying that aside from the murders, Washington had one of the lowest crime rates in the country.

Responsibility is a key mark of maturity and is basic to stewardship of the gifts we have received from God. But responsibility has a seductive side and may become irresponsibility under a mask. Taking too much responsibility—in other words, assuming responsibility that isn't ours—can be just as harmful as taking too little.

We rarely get criticized for taking too much responsibility; rather, we are often praised for it.

In *The Road Less Traveled*, psychiatrist Scott Peck describes taking too little responsibility as a character disorder and taking too much as a neurosis. A typical problem he saw in his patients was assuming too much responsibility and then complaining of the stress it caused. Poet William Blake had a word for this pattern: "mind-forged manacles."

What are some examples of over-responsibility or misplaced responsibility? A caring person might assume the medical care of an uncle who has children of his own. This begins in charity but may end in frustration and anger on the part of the caregiver (and the children). Or a pastor might devote so much energy and time to convincing uninterested parishioners to come to a Wednesday night discussion that he ends up having a stroke. Much energy is wasted on stewing about things beyond one's control: the weather, government spending, the spread of cancer, the conduct of grown children or grandchildren. Stories about the fallout of over-responsibility are regularly in the news: a man who destroyed his marriage because of total commitment to Little League sports; a woman who gave a vast fortune to protecting a rare species of fish, which died out shortly after her death.

The mature person is responsible, neither under-responsible nor over-responsible. Pope John XXIII, a very wise and mature person with a monumental assignment, described his approach to problems brought to him daily in these words: "I try to see everything: I overlook most, and change what I can." He knew that even though he was responsible for leading the church, he was not God, and most things were beyond his control. He discerned which issues needed his attention and trusted God to take care of the rest. Mother Teresa didn't worry about whether her work with the dying poor was judged successful: "God does not ask me to be successful, but faithful."

We are often over-responsible toward ourselves. "I know it's wrong for me to feel this way." Yet a feeling is not wrong. My responsibility lies in what I do about the feeling, in my actions and attitudes. "I feel terrible because I have so many distractions when I try to pray." Distractions are by definition involuntary. They are not my responsibility unless I make them voluntary.

In a business (or a parish or a religious community) an over-responsible person may take on unassigned jobs until he is overwhelmed and stressed, and probably angry. But even when offered relief, he may be unable to let go. A person with a big job may be unable to delegate part of the responsibility. "I am the only one who can do this right." All roads stop at his door, and he is very angry as a result.

In the spiritual realm, under-responsibility is associated with the sin of presumption, and over- or misplaced responsibility, with a lack of faith. God will not or cannot take care of things, and therefore I must. The call to commitment and faithfulness does not mean that we agree to do everything or that we refuse to do enough. It means we discern the true responsibility within the daily demands, needs, and opportunities that come our way. This is the road to charity, joy, and peace.

A Lesson from the Desert

In the rare case that you don't have firsthand experience of it yourself, editorial writers and social commentators will tell you that our society is experiencing a proliferation of lawsuits on a scale unimaginable by any other society in history.

The need for insurance protection increases daily. Things that were presumed innocent before, like having glass panes in your house windows or leaving your car unlocked, may be a source of liability for you rather than for an intruder. Some attorneys now even advertise their ability to sue and, subtly or not so subtly, encourage us to look for reasons.

An unfortunate by-product of this litigation fever is the creation of an atmosphere of mistrust and suspicion, as if everyone is checking on our exposed liability, or a mood of criticism and judgment and a desire to take advantage. The German language has the expressive term *Schadenfreude*, which means "malicious pleasure," glee at the discomfort or tragedy of another.

Behind all this lurks what the early monks of the Egyptian desert, our ancestors, would have called a demon: the demon of condemnation. They understood one of the foremost perverting passions of the human heart to be a judgmental attitude, looking through the lens of a one-person judge and jury to condemn the actions of others. As long as you are consumed by this, they said, you cannot be converted and saved. They called on Scripture as witness: "Stop judging, that you may not be judged" (Matt 7:1); "Who are you to pass judgment on someone else's servant?" (Rom 14:4).

Perhaps a dose of early Christianity from the desert would be a helpful antidote to our present rush to judgment. I think particularly of the example and teaching of Abba Ammonas, a fourth-century disciple of Anthony the Great, renowned for his patience and holiness and wisdom. Two stories especially reveal his spirit. "It happened that a brother of evil reputation was observed taking a woman into his tent. The dwellers of that place gathered together to chase the brother from his cell, and they asked Abba Ammonas to join them. When the brother inside heard of this, he hid the woman in a large cask. As the visitors entered, Abba Ammonas perceived the situation, but for the sake of God he kept the secret: he entered, seated himself on the cask, and when they found nothing, said, 'What is this? May God forgive you for this accusation!' After praying he dismissed the visitors, then taking the brother by the hand said, 'Brother, be on your guard.' With these words, he withdrew."

And the second: "Someone brought to Abba Ammonas a young unmarried girl who was pregnant, saying, 'Give this sinner a penance.' But he, having marked the young girl's womb with the sign of the cross, commanded that six pairs of fine linen sheets should be given her, saying, 'It is for fear that when she comes to give birth she may die, and there will be nothing for a decent burial.' Her accusers were angry. 'Why did you do that? Give her a punishment.' Abba Ammonas replied, 'Look, brothers, she is near death; what am I to do?' Then he sent her away, and no one dared accuse anyone anymore."

Abba Ammonas might be considered crazy today, or at least irresponsible. But he did not fear to live by the gospel, trusting that there is a judge who relieves us of the responsibility to condemn others. He did not deny the sins of those who were brought to him, but neither did he consider condemnation the way to healing; and he feared a possibly more incurable sin in the heart of the accusers, whether they were right or wrong in their judgment.

People today often make a nervous joke of holiness and imply in various ways that they are not comfortable with the concept, perhaps because in some way they associate holiness with severity and are afraid that the holy person will see through them and lash out in judgment.

True holiness is just the opposite. It is loving and tolerant and hopeful about people, no matter how far they fall in their weakness. In other words, it imitates God.

This was the way the desert generation understood holiness. As they said of Abba Ammonas, "He advanced to the point where his goodness was so great, he took no notice of wickedness."

The Turtle on the Fencepost

A few years ago a philosophy professor at the University of Texas was approached after class by one of his students. The student complained that the professor had mentioned moral law in his lecture, but that another teacher had convinced him during the previous semester that there isn't any moral law.

"Every society makes up its own right and wrong, its own good and bad, its own fair and unfair—and each one makes up something different."

The professor answered: "I'm glad to hear you say that, because I'm lazy and hate to grade papers. At the end of this semester I'll be able to save myself some work by giving you an F without looking at your papers at all. Since you don't believe in moral standards like fairness that are true for everyone, I know you won't object. We make up our morals as we go. We don't have to be bound by arbitrary standards."

Faced with this dire application of his own theory, the student was quick to see and to admit that there are universal moral standards that all people implicitly and preconsciously agree on; these standards have important application every day. People of all ages and places share an innate sense of right and wrong. It can be manipulated, shaded, or denied, but it is there to start with.

Cardinal Newman found this universal sense of right and wrong, the existence of a conscience in every human being, to be the most powerful argument for the existence of God, or at least of a reality beyond this world that affects its creatures intimately—a proof more universally convincing than philosophical arguments about the first cause or prime mover, the size of creation or its beauties and powers. Where does this internal monitor come from? It is not necessary to life in this world. No other creatures have a sense of right and wrong, and so no anxiety about doing good or evil, no premeditation, no judgment, and no guilt. All human beings, however, have a sense of right and wrong that causes us to ponder and agonize in our decisions and to deal with the good or bad that we do. This isn't part of our natural makeup as creatures of this physical world. It had to come from somewhere, and of its nature it had to come from someone; in other words an intelligence is behind it.

This is an application of what is known as the turtle-on-the-fencepost argument. If you spot a turtle stationed on a fencepost, you know (barring a flood) it can't have gotten there by itself. An outside agent has been at work. This is the principle used in the search for intelligent life elsewhere in the universe. Scientific instruments focused on outer space are listening for patterned signals that would indicate an intelligent source.

If a sense of right and wrong is present in only one form of life on this earth, and present consistently in that form, this is evidence of an intelligent agent affecting us and setting our moral boundaries from outside the closed system of the visible world. We may call this agent a higher power, an external force, or God. But we can't ignore its existence, because the proof is everywhere there are people. We carry the proof within us.

Halos and Dark Nights

In October 2003, six years after her death, Mother Teresa of Calcutta was beatified by Pope John Paul II. The process usually takes much longer than that—decades, even centuries. But for no one since Pope John XXIII had there been such a universal recognition of sanctity and an appeal for church approbation. An intense investigation of Mother Teresa's life has been made, beginning with her birth as Agnes Bojaxhiu in Albania in 1910, through her life as a missionary Sister of Loreto and then her labor as foundress of the Missionaries of Charity among the poorest of the poor, until her death in 1997.

The Congregation for the Causes of Saints investigates carefully to be sure there are no secrets that would cast doubt on the fidelity of the holy person. In Mother Teresa's case, there were no such surprises, but there was a surprise of a different sort, which has made the effect of her witness even more profound.

In letters written to her spiritual directors, beginning shortly after the founding of the Missionaries of Charity in 1947, she describes an interior life of spiritual darkness that continued until her death. After an intense experience of Christ's presence during the time of the calling to her new mission in 1946 and 1947, the feelings of peace, union, and love ceased. While she carried on her work among the poor, radiating such conviction and joy that the whole world was warmed, she herself was feeling loneliness and abandonment. She persisted in raw faith, strengthened by the daily hour of prayer before the Blessed Sacrament, which is at the center of the religious observance of her community. All the while she was suffering intensely, describing "that terrible pain of loss, of God not wanting me, of God not being God, of God not really existing."

Commentators have noted how similar this experience is to that of her namesake, St. Therese of Lisieux, who died exactly one hundred years earlier. Therese struck the world by the warm and intimate picture of her early relationship with Christ portrayed in *The Story of a Soul*, but her witness has become even more compelling by the discovery that she spent the last eighteen months to two years of her short life, during the illness that ended in her death, experiencing nothing but spiritual darkness and alienation. She confessed that she could finally understand the appeals of both atheism and suicide.

These saints may be seen as God's special gifts to our age, where so many people experience not only questions about their relationship to God and feelings of dryness and emptiness, but also radical doubt even about God's existence as they are confronted on all sides by the contemporary "wisdom" of secularism and materialism. Here are two saints who experienced the same emptiness, which they confronted without wavering in their conviction of God's presence and love. This became a means of their purification; they were emptied out and filled with Christ, and through them blessings now flow to the world, visibly in the form of miracles and other blessings, invisibly in gifts of spiritual purification and renewal.

They both reached out to help people during their own agony, like Jesus ministering to the desolate women on his way to Calvary: Mother Teresa on the streets of Calcutta, bathing the wounds of the dying; St. Therese enclosed in her convent, loving the sisters in her community.

The Surprise of Mother Teresa

In August 2007, *Time* magazine published a cover story for the tenth anniversary of the death of Mother Teresa, revealing that during the years of her renowned ministry as a servant of Christ to the poor she had experienced an almost unrelieved interior darkness. This was not new information—Catholic News Service had reported it in 2002—but the news sent a shock wave inside and outside the church. Shortly afterward, a book of her spiritual letters and other writings was published by Father Brian Kolodiejchuk, MC, the postulator of her cause for sainthood and a member of the religious order she founded.

Reactions in the media were generally respectful; but there were, on the one side, defenders of Mother Teresa who downplayed her spiritual darkness as poetic exaggeration and, on the other, those who interpreted it as a sign of her self-deception or, worse, dishonesty in playing a fraudulent role.

But there is no sign of fraud in what Mother Teresa reported (which, by the way, she didn't intend for the world's eyes); rather, it underscores the integrity of a life of deep faith. We had been impressed by her selfless ministry, her dedication to prayer, her witness to gospel values on the streets of Calcutta and in the halls of government. She was a force for good wherever she went. The gift she has given us after her death is more precious and will be more effective for good than all that the world experienced from her during her life.

As a young member of the missionary Sisters of Our Lady of Loreto, Sister Teresa was committed, happy, and effective in her religious life and her ministry of education. She was not looking for something different, but she began experiencing vivid communications from Jesus calling her to a new ministry, one that would require her to give up her present life and work and relationships. "I want Indian Missionary Sisters of Charity," he said to her, "who would be my fire of love among the very poor—the sick—the dying—the little street children." During the time of discernment with her community and through all the canonical issues and explanations, she felt Jesus very close to her. But soon after she stepped out into the streets of Calcutta with no clear plans of how she would accomplish the new mission for Jesus, the warmth of this intimacy ceased. With the exception of one short period, she did not experience spiritual consolation during the fifty years that followed.

Spiritual darkness is nothing new in the history of Christian spirituality. The phrase "dark night of the soul" from St. John of the Cross is so familiar that it is used loosely today to label any time of difficulty. But John describes the dark night of the soul as an extreme kind of divine purification given only to very few. What is more common is the experience he called a "dark night of the senses," a painful time of spiritual dryness and emptiness, which might last weeks or even months, but usually not years. God remains present in all of these trials, though without relieving the sense of loss and separation and meaninglessness. The dark night of the soul is not a sign that God does not love the individual, just the opposite; God is offering chosen disciples the opportunity to be completely emptied of self-will and self-centeredness, and to be filled with the grace of interior freedom. Only a few with intense trust in and desire for God have the spiritual strength to hold on during this purification. This was evident one hundred years ago in St. Therese of Lisieux and more recently in Blessed Teresa of Calcutta.

Now we know what was really going on in the life of Mother Teresa and it is a gift to us. Her public image was of someone who was very good and was being rewarded for it by the warmth of God's closeness in her life. When we saw her pictured in prayer, we didn't realize she had the same struggles we have to remain focused amid distractions, to remain faithful to the daily time of prayer without the props of spiritual feelings. When she smiled, we thought it was because she felt happy, deeply at peace, but it was because of her unyielding conviction in the loving presence of Christ, despite her sense of his absence. She did not have a head start on any of us but was actually struggling as hard as anyone. Her radiance was not a charade but a spiritual reality coming from deep inside her, where her daily dying to self was giving birth to the resurrected life of Christ. She continued this to the end of her life and now, as with all the saints, the heart she opened to God has become a special channel of grace for those who are still seeking God here on earth. An author of books on the saints said that the evidence of her secret struggle reveals Mother Teresa to be "one of the greatest of the saints."

Mother Teresa gives us new hope for our own struggle to be faithful. She seemed to be above us, to be swept up in a mystical union while bending down to serve the dying poor. Now we know that she was going forward in darkness, not coasting on a kind of spiritual cloud but driven from the inside by an intense love and desire for God who was her only light.

A Monastic Doctor of the Church

In October 1997, the centenary of St. Therese of Lisieux's death, Pope John Paul II named her the thirty-third Doctor of the Church. Doctor in this sense means teacher; the designation identifies certain saints as contributing particularly important insights into the mystery of faith and the Christian life.

This title for the Little Flower would have seemed strange not too long ago. Although she has been a popular and powerful intercessor among Catholic faithful almost since the day of her death in 1897, for most of that time we knew her only through a filtered image. Her biographers presented her as pure and holy, yes, but naive and saccharine as well, a saint who was lifted out of the world before she had experienced the hardships and real questions of life.

The biographers meant well, but the distortion limited St. Therese's appeal and her broader effectiveness in the church. Since the 1950s this has changed. Therese has emerged as the same pure and holy person, but one who wrestled with the major questions raised by the scientific age, including atheism—one whose intense physical and mental suffering gave her an insight into the temptation to suicide, and who lived her last two years in a "dark night" without spiritual consolation.

But she was not named a Doctor for these reasons. Her contributions as a teacher of the church are in two main areas: the living of the faith and the place of prayer in the mission of the church.

Therese described her journey to holiness as a "little way," a way of finding God in each moment as it comes along, accepting and responding to the unraveling of daily reality as a gift and call from God. This little way makes the heights of sanctity accessible to all people, whatever their rank or personal gifts.

As simple as this sounds, it is of monumental importance, and its full articulation as the "universal call to holiness" was one of the achievements of the Second Vatican Council. At the time Therese lived, high holiness was perceived as out of reach except to chosen souls, usually those with religious vocations; most people were hoping for sneak-in-the-door salvation. Therese also scotched the notion, as later also would Vatican II, that holiness relies on our efforts rather than God's.

In this teaching, Therese was enriching and refining from her own experience a post-Reformation renewal of lay spirituality initiated by St. Francis de Sales (d. 1622), an earlier Doctor, and embellished by Brother Lawrence of the Resurrection (d. 1691) and Father Jean-Pierre de Caussade (d. 1751). She contributed her insight into this doctrine and fashioned a method of living it out that would be understandable and accessible for people of the modern age.

Her other major contribution concerns prayer and mission. In a startling declaration in 1927, Pope Pius XI put St. Therese on an equal footing with St. Francis Xavier by naming her co-patron of missions: an enclosed Carmelite praying in her cell paired with a Jesuit missionary evangelizing India and Japan by land and sea. In a teaching that should be of immense significance to all of us in the limited scope of our daily lives, but particularly to the sick and shut-ins, the church says that prayer in the silence of the heart is as important to the church's mission as hands-on ministry in the field.

Therese understood her vocation to be a missionary of love far beyond the confines of her cloister through opening her heart to the people in her daily life and through her prayer: "Love appeared to me as the hinge for my vocation. . . . I knew that the Church had a heart and that such a heart appeared to be aflame with love. I knew that one love drove the members of the Church to action, that if this love were extinguished the apostles would have proclaimed the gospel no longer, the martyrs would have shed their blood no more."

She saw divine love as the force powering the work of salvation in the world and understood that by letting that love be released through herself by the channel especially of a life consistent with her prayer, she was fulfilling her missionary vocation. In this way, she gave modern focus to an ancient monastic insight, expressed a few hundred years earlier by *The Cloud of Unknowing*: "I tell you this, one loving blind desire for God alone is more valuable in itself, more pleasing to God and to the saints, more beneficial to your own growth, and more helpful to your friends, both living and dead, than anything else you could do" (9).

The recognition of St. Therese's teaching should be of great help and consolation to all of us. Life is so complicated, and the proliferation of information and knowledge so staggering, that we can feel helpless, lost, and unimportant. This especially affects those of us limited by age, disability, lack of education, or economic hardship. What can we do? What do we matter?

Yet the church tells us that Christ's mission depends on those such as us. We can be holy right where we are, and become channels of Christ's love worldwide. By making Therese a Doctor, the church is saying that in heaven's view the Little Flower is not little and neither is her "little way."

Mary and Peter in the Church

"The Church's structure is totally ordered to the holiness of Christ's members," stated Pope John Paul II in his 1988 apostolic letter, On the Dignity and Vocation of Women, "and holiness is measured according to the great mystery in which the Bride responds with the gift of love to the gift of the Bridegroom" (27). We are that Bride, Jesus is our Bridegroom. The first of us to respond was Mary, and she did so wholeheartedly: "Mary of Nazareth . . . 'precedes' everyone on the path to holiness; in her person 'the church has already reached that perfection whereby she exists without spot or wrinkle'" (cf. Eph 5:29) (27). The Catechism summarizes: "This is why the Marian dimension of the Church precedes the Petrine [that of St. Peter]" (773).

The Marian and the Petrine: what does that mean? The role of Peter in the church, the "apostolic and Petrine" role, is that of governance. It is expressed in the hierarchical structure of the church. The Marian dimension is the response of human love to divine love, the dimension of personal holiness. In her total self-gift to God, Mary is the "figure" of the church, preceding all other disciples on the path of holiness.

To say that the Marian dimension of the church precedes the Petrine simply means that all the institutions of the church, including the hierarchical structure of pope and bishops, exist to promote the holiness of the members (including, of course, the pope and bishops). "All are called to respond—as a bride—with the gift of their lives to the inexpressible gift of the love of Christ" (On the Dignity and Vocation of Women, 27). This is the true exercise of the "royal priesthood," presenting oneself as a "living sacrifice, holy and pleasing to God" (Rom 12:1). The Catechism says that the communion of the faithful with God is "the purpose which governs everything" in the church (773).

The leadership structure of the church is presented here as a servant and a liberating force for the search for personal holiness. That it may not be so in every instance does not cancel its role. There are Christians who believe there should be no human authority between the individual believer and God. History has shown how acting on that principle has splintered the Body of Christ. We need the Petrine dimension, present from the earliest days of the church, to make the way clear for the Marian dimension: "I exhort the presbyters among you, as a fellow presbyter and witness to the sufferings of Christ and one who has a share in the glory to be revealed. Tend the flock of God in your midst, [overseeing] not by constraint but willingly" (1 Pet 5:1-2). Saint Paul brings the two dimensions together in his greeting to the community at Philippi: "To all the saints in Christ Jesus who are in Philippi, with the bishops and deacons" (Phil 1:1, NRSV). The leaders' mission is to so teach and arrange things in the church that the holy ones may walk with confidence on the path of holiness in Christ, the Petrine dimension serving the Marian.

What does this mean for you and me? Every Christian belongs to the primary dimension of the church, the Marian. Sometimes we think the leadership and ministerial roles are primary. But "[t]he Marian dimension of the Church precedes the Petrine." The higher visibility of leadership roles in the church makes it inevitable that the hierarchy and those in ordained ministry will sometimes be thought to be on a higher plane of membership. Newspaper reports even equate the leadership with "the church." But the church in the primary dimension is all of us who make up the Body of Christ, sharing the call and following the lead of Mary, the first disciple.

Both the Marian and the Petrine dimensions are essential to the life of the church of Christ. If the Marian dimension ignores the Petrine, error is sure to follow; if the Petrine ignores the Marian, sin is sure to follow. We need to be attentive to and concerned about both dimensions. But our primary concern, wherever God has called us in the life of the church, is to respond as Mary did, with a heart full of love, every day.

The Disciple and the Mother

The gospels of Matthew and Mark place three women at the foot of Jesus' cross on Calvary: Mary Magdalene, Mary the mother of James and Joseph, and Salome.

Luke identifies no one by name. John has a different scene: besides Mary Magdalene and the other Mary, there are the mother of Jesus and an unnamed beloved disciple.

Debate has raged off and on for the last couple of centuries about the identity of the beloved disciple. The traditional solution had been to identify him with the apostle John, the fourth evangelist, attributing to his humility the fact that he never mentions himself by name.

The reason this identification is not totally satisfying is because of the nature of the Gospel of John. For one thing, there is clear evidence that the document passed through several hands before arriving at its final form. Also, the gospel often operates on more than one level: it is known for irony, double entendre, and symbolism. Maybe John did not mention his own name because of humility, but why didn't he mention the name of the mother of Jesus? There are other Marys in the gospel, but we would never know from John that this was the name of Jesus' mother, though she is mentioned prominently both at Cana (John 2:1-12) and at the cross (John 19:25-27). Further, both times, instead of addressing her as mother, Jesus calls her "Woman," a disturbingly impersonal title by today's standards.

Other figures in the gospel, both named and unnamed, frequently have symbolic meaning beyond their literal identity. Nicodemus (John 3:1-21) represents the faithful Jew; the woman at the well (John 4:1-42), the misguided but openhearted seeker; the man born blind (9:1-34), Lazarus (11:1-44), and Mary of Bethany (12:1-8), in various ways the reborn Christian disciple.

By not naming the mother of Jesus and the beloved disciple, and by bringing them together for an important dialogue at the foot of the cross, the evangelist signals that here too are persons with meaning beyond their personal identities.

Mary's special role in the Fourth Gospel is signaled at her first appearance, the wedding at Cana. Commentators have noted that the Gospel of John begins with the first words of Genesis, "In the beginning . . .," and then parallels the seven days of the original creation with seven days of a new creation, climaxing on the seventh day at the wedding feast of Cana. Jesus' address of his mother as "Woman," an unusual though not disrespectful usage, connects her to the woman of the first creation, Eve, the "mother of all the living" (Gen 3:20). Mary is obviously the new Eve, the woman of the new creation, the mother of all those living a new life.

Mary appears at the foot of the cross with the beloved disciple both in her own person and in her symbolic role. "When Jesus saw his mother and the disciple there whom he loved, he said to his mother, 'Woman, behold, your son.' Then he said to the disciple, 'Behold, your mother.'" The disciple recognized that from now on there would be an intimate relationship between himself and the mother of Jesus: "And from that hour the disciple took her into his home" (John 19:26-27).

One main issue separating Catholics today from many other Christians is the place accorded to the mother of Jesus in the practice of the faith. This was not an immediate fruit of the Reformation but resulted as every traditional practice was subjected to questioning. The later Reformers contended that the special role of Mary has no foundation in Scripture and that Catholic Marian theology is a production of medieval piety some centuries later.

The scene at the foot of the cross in John's gospel, however, in the light of that gospel's presentation of the mother of Jesus and the beloved disciple, shows that the special role of Mary is highlighted right in the heart of the New Testament and right at the moment of salvation: "Woman, behold, your son. . . . Behold, your mother."

It is also a misreading of the historical evidence to suggest that Marian piety developed only in the Middle Ages. Certainly many of the devotions of popular piety date from then and later. But Christian writers give witness to the special role of Mary from the earliest times. The first title they give her, from the second century on, is the very title implied in the Gospel of John, the "new Eve," which recognizes Mary in God's design as "the mother of all the new-living."

In this case, the study of Scripture with the tools of modern scholarship, rather than breaking new ground, has confirmed the interpretation and insights of the first generations of Christian believers. We are finally getting the point (again) why the mother of Jesus and the beloved disciple are left unnamed in the Gospel of John. They have a significance beyond their personal identities. The mother of Jesus is given to us as our mother in the life of faith. This confirms our Catholic tradition that Mary's unique role in salvation does not detract from the role of Christ but is an integral part of the gospel message.

Empowered by the Word of God

A few years ago, in connection with a meeting of North American Benedictine Superiors in Mexico, I was blessed with an opportunity to accompany Benedictine sisters of the Guadalupe Missionary community to places of ministry in distressed areas in and around Cuernavaca.

We visited a neighborhood where fifteen young and middle-aged mothers banded together in a small cooperative to make children's clothing and embroidered goods that they take turns selling in the streets. They do this to supplement the inadequate earnings of their husbands in order to feed their children. This takes courage every day because the society is against women's initiatives outside the home, and because the local government requires exorbitant vending fees that the women cannot pay.

A few years ago, when things seemed hopeless, one of the sisters began to gather these women for mutual support of one another. She had them come together regularly to pray and read the Bible, to listen to the word of God and discern its meaning. They became aware of God's presence among them, of their own dignity and worth in God's sight, and they received confidence to help one another emerge from their darkness.

Individually they can give only a few hours a week for this time away from their families. They cover for one another and respond to needs in the various families. The strength for this, they told us, continues to come from the prayerful sharing of the word of God in their regular weekly gathering.

We also heard a report from adult and youth Bible reflection groups who are impelled by the teaching of Jesus, St. Paul, and the prophets to look beyond their own troubles to serve the needs of others. A teen told of her bus trip of many hours to Chiapas in southeastern Mexico, where the government had instituted a systematic program to push the indigenous Indians off their oil-rich land. She said it was dangerous work—"I might lose my leather (skin)"—but had to be done.

The oppressive conditions in Chiapas have attracted worldwide attention; but the struggle is far from over. Only constant accompaniment of the Indians by Mexicans from other parts of the country and by international human rights volunteers keeps the army from smothering the native groups. A network of Catholic Bible study groups across Mexico has organized into twelve sections, each responsible for sending representatives to Chiapas one month of the year to provide a protective presence among the Indians. Two or three times a month army operatives single out youth leaders for harassment, sometimes beating the males and raping the females. Disappearances are also common. Still, volunteers keep rallying to the need. The afternoon I was to leave, two of the Benedictine sisters left on a long bus ride to spend several days "walking with" endangered coffee harvesters.

Even our own group experienced a little of the muscle the world can bring to bear on those who would counteract its injustice. One of the scheduled speakers at our meeting was Mother Irene Dabalus, OSB, prioress general of the Tutzing Missionary Benedictines. At the last minute she was unable to obtain a visa from the Mexican government which, as a citizen of the Philippines, she was required to have. The explanation was that the national government is very reluctant to grant visas to religious leaders, including Catholic bishops, because of the publicity that might be given to a critique of human rights violations.

All of us are helpless before worldly might, but what overcomes the world is faith (1 John 5:4). The word of God helps to build faith, whether in Chiapas or in the U.S., and empowers from within.

Joy in Honduras

In March 2006 I joined an eight-day mission to Trujillo, Honduras, organized by Christ the King Church in Little Rock, Arkansas. This ninth Honduras mission of the parish had ninety volunteers to staff several medical clinics, teach and evangelize, and conduct construction and maintenance projects. It was a graced time for everyone.

Veterans of the mission had told me how wonderful the people were and that, no matter what their personal misery or poverty, they always seemed to be happy. After I had been there a couple days, I understood what they meant, but I was a little bit uneasy with that way of describing the attitude of the Honduran people and couldn't put my finger on the reason why.

After a few more days on the mission, it dawned on me that "happy" was not the right word. It doesn't take experience or maturity or even knowledge of one's situation to be happy. A baby is happy when dry and well-fed, and unhappy when wet and hungry. Happiness in that sense comes from the outside and is determined by circumstances. The proper description of the attitude of most people we encountered in the clinic lines was joy. Joy comes from the inside and is a decision about life and its meaning. Only a mature person has the wherewithal to be joyful.

The Honduran people we met were usually poor and often sick. Parents brought children who had maladies they couldn't treat, some simple and some complex. They weren't happy in a giggly sense. They knew how bad it was. They knew the unfairness of the distribution of goods in this world; they knew that we visitors had it much better in our country than they had in theirs. They knew but they still could smile. But they weren't smiling because they were naive, an assumption one might make when coming from a very different setting, one in which sickness and poverty are less visible.

One of the things that made me sense I was in a different country, more than the terrain and the climate, was the absence of whining. The people in the villages possessed very little and many things were working against them, but they weren't whining. In the United States, where most of us have everything we want and more than we need, we whine constantly. We look around for someone to blame when things don't go our way.

Someone remarked that though the children who came to the clinics often needed an examination or treatment that involved pain, only the babies cried out if they were given a shot or otherwise hurt. The older ones felt it, but expected it, and didn't blame anybody for it. Pain was part of the price for healing. This was another piece of evidence which told me I was in a different world. In our culture, pain is no longer a natural part of life. Pain is unfair. There should be a pill or an injection to protect me from pain or to rescue me from it, and I will lash out, maybe even sue, if I don't get relief on time. For the Hondurans we met, pain was still a natural ingredient of living. If it happened, they didn't automatically look for someone to blame. They accepted it and moved on. Something external was not going to tell them how to live their lives.

But there was also plenty of happiness in Honduras, for all of us, especially because of the miracles of modern medicine. Over 5,000 people received some kind of individual medical attention, from very serious surgeries to routine examinations. Our hearts were in our throats when, for example, a simple procedure (simple in this country) permitted a child to hear her mother's voice for the first time, and when the face of a boy lit up with delight when a specially constructed walker enabled him to maneuver without help for the first time.

Any meeting is an exchange of gifts. Paul expressed this when looking forward to his visit to the Romans: "I long to see you, that I may share with you some spiritual gift so that you may be strengthened, that is, that you and I may be mutually encouraged by one another's faith, yours and mine" (Rom 1:11-12). On a medical mission like ours, what is going on seems clear: we are the givers, they are the receivers. But that is a deceptive reading of the situation, as we all knew even before the mission. Afterward, members of the team spoke of receiving more from the Hondurans than they had given. Individuals would have different ways of explaining what they meant by that, but I think all of us in one way or another were uplifted by the joy in the hearts of the people who were waiting for us in Honduras.

The Gift of the Resurrection

The feast of Easter is the central event of the church year, the solemnity of solemnities. Easter is every Christian's birthday in the faith, even for those who were baptized on some other day of the year. We mark it by beginning again, renewing the promises of our baptism. The church knows that we cannot celebrate this feast of our redemption adequately on one day, so we have an octave of Easter—eight days as one long day—and a Paschal season of fifty days ending with the feast of Pentecost.

It may be more proper to say that the Paschal season reaches its climax in the feast of Pentecost, for Pentecost celebrates the giving of the Holy Spirit, the "first gift to those who believe" (Fourth Eucharistic Prayer), the essential gift won for us by the resurrection of Christ.

To the woman at the well, Jesus spoke of the Spirit as a fountain of living water, "welling up to eternal life" (John 4:14). Sometime later, at the feast of Tabernacles in Jerusalem, he called this gift "Rivers of living water, [flowing] from within" (John 7:38), and the evangelist commented: "He said this in reference to the Spirit that those who came to believe in him were to receive. There was, of course, no Spirit yet, because Jesus had not yet been glorified" (John 7:39). The Spirit, in other words, could not be given before the resurrection.

Why was this? Wasn't Jesus always united to the Holy Spirit as the Son of God? True, and Luke's gospel emphasizes that Jesus' conception (1:35), his ministry (4:18), and even his time of temptation (4:1-2) were under the influence of the Spirit. But the limitations of his mission as the incarnate Savior prevented him from pouring out the gift of the Spirit for universal salvation. In God's plan, it was through the resurrection, by which Jesus was exalted and his body suffused with heavenly glory, that the Spirit was made available as the source of our salvation.

Jesus' resurrection was not a return to this life, as in the case of Lazarus (John 11:1-44). Lazarus's resurrection was a miracle, but only a temporary reprieve from death. The resurrection of Jesus is in a completely different order. He was not "brought back to life" by the Father but, rather, broke through death by divine power to a new and permanent form of life: now "he lives for God" (Rom 6:10). And in this victory he won salvation for us. His body became glorified, the Spirit bursting its limitations, and from that moment the Spirit was and is poured out everywhere in full measure.

This is why the resurrection is crucial to our redemption. Eternal life is in us by the working of the Holy Spirit; it is the presence of the Spirit in us. Without this Holy Spirit, there would be no living of Christ's life, no sacraments, no church. We would be earthbound, unable to hope for heavenly life. But when Jesus' body was flooded with the blinding light of God's glory in the resurrection, his humanity became the eternal instrument of salvation from which the gift of the Spirit pours.

Saint Paul sees in the resurrection the beginning of a new world order: through the resurrection, Christ has achieved "new creation" (Gal 6:15). The Christian is urged to start absolutely new without anything left over from the past: "For our paschal lamb, Christ, has been sacrificed. Therefore let us celebrate the feast, not with the old yeast, the yeast of malice and wickedness, but with the unleavened bread of sincerity and truth" (1 Cor 5:7). In the Synoptic Gospels, the severing with the past is symbolized by the splitting of the temple veil (Matt 27:51; Mark 15:38; Luke 23:45). The earth itself responded in storm clouds, darkness, and earthquake. Early Christian theology at times spoke of the resurrection as the "real" birth of Christ as savior (Acts 13:33).

The resurrection of Jesus happened historically, but because of the gift of the resurrection, the Spirit, it does not belong to the past. The Christian life is lived in the permanent moment of the resurrection. The New Testament is full of the excitement this realization brings: "Blessed be the God and Father of our Lord Jesus Christ, who in his great mercy gave us a new birth to a living hope through the resurrection of Jesus Christ from the dead" (1 Pet 1:3). "For God who said, 'Let light shine out of darkness,' has shone in our hearts to bring to light the knowledge of the glory of God on the face of [Jesus] Christ" (2 Cor 4:6). "[H]ope does not disappoint, because the love of God has been poured out into our hearts by the holy Spirit who has been given to us" (Rom 5:5).

Prayer:
To See as God Sees

Holy Seeing

"Blessed are your eyes, because they see." "Blessed are the eyes that see what you see." These two sayings of Jesus are almost the same, but not quite. The first appears in Matthew's gospel (13:16), the second, in Luke's (10:23). The second is better remembered because it has an object—"what you see"— which is Jesus himself, and is easier to understand. The first one almost doesn't make sense. Your eyes see what?

In its place in Matthew's gospel the saying does make sense: Jesus is explaining his use of parables. Some do not understand them—"They look but do not see"—but the disciples do understand. The object of "see" in this case is the meaning of the parables. Blessed are the eyes of those who understand the kingdom of God.

They have, in other words, been given the grace to see things the way God sees them, which is really seeing. Not everyone sees the same thing the same way. Witnesses to an accident may give quite different reports. After a storm one will be struck by the clouds, another by the rainbow. In the same person one will see a wasted life, another a child of God. The crowd saw in Levi a despised tax collector, but Jesus saw a man hungry for God.

To contemporary author Steven Covey we owe the axiom: "We see the world not as it is, but as we are." In an important sense, becoming a disciple of Jesus is learning to see the world as Jesus sees it, as God sees it. Saint Paul talks about "put[ting] on the Lord Jesus Christ" (Rom 13:14) and having "the mind of Christ" (1 Cor 2:16). In teaching us to see, Jesus created stories about people who had this kind of vision—the Good Samaritan looking at the man in the ditch, the loving father looking at his returning prodigal son—as well as about those who weren't able really to see, like the rich man overlooking the beggar at his gate.

An ancient monastic practice recovered in our day focuses on learning how to see the world as God sees it, to view reality from the divine perspective. It is called *lectio divina*, which literally means divine or holy reading. This is a way of putting on the mind of God by absorbing the word of God, letting the divine Scriptures penetrate deeply so that we may be transformed by divine grace. In its most familiar form this means a slow and repetitive brooding over the biblical text, but it is not an intellectual exercise, a form of Scripture study. "Reading" in this practice from Christian antiquity is not a fast and aggressive accumulation of information, in which we try to devour what is in a text and then move on, but a process belonging to a time when books were copied by hand and were scarce and expensive. Divine reading is more like sitting with the holy word to let its priorities and point of view seep into us: to begin to see the universe and all that is in it from God's point of view, to look on everything and everyone with love. This spiritual exercise always leads to prayer.

Lectio divina has unfortunately been confused in the contemporary renewal with another important religious exercise, spiritual reading, which has a different purpose. Spiritual reading is reading about the doctrine of the faith, its history and application, and for information and inspiration. Its realm is sacred theology, the nature and practice of prayer, the lives of the saints. Spiritual reading is a necessary background for an informed spiritual life and is a form of study. *Lectio divina* is at all points either prayer or leading to prayer, more of the heart than of the head. Its goal is not information but transformation. It might be better to call the practice "holy seeing" rather than holy reading.

We need both of these practices for a sound spirituality: spiritual reading, which provides a context of sound doctrine and information and awakens our desire for God, and the daily communion with God in prayer, whether it is in *lectio divina* or some other practice. One beauty of *lectio divina* is that it can incorporate prayer from its most vocal or verbal expressions to the most silent and contemplative.

Learning to see reality as God sees it is not some external exercise, like acquiring a new skill. It is a process of conversion, becoming more and more God-centered and God-filled. We are amazed at the stories of saints who were able to see the face of God in everyone, even their torturers. In this they were exactly like Jesus. Thomas Merton made this point about saints: "The saints are what they are, not because their sanctity makes them admirable to others, but because the gift of sainthood makes it possible for them to admire everybody else. It gives them a clarity of compassion that can find good in the most terrible criminals. It delivers them from the burden of judging others, condemning others. It teaches them to bring the good out of others by compassion, mercy and pardon."

"We see the world not as it is, but as we are."

God's DVD Library

One of the first things I am going to do when I get to heaven is ask about the use of God's DVD library. I won't be asking for access to any restricted files on people's private lives, but only for the DVDs in the General Use category. What I'm interested in are not secrets (or at least will not be secrets at that point) but a chance for an eyewitness view of great events I've wondered about.

Some of these DVDs will answer questions but most, I expect, will simply reveal in greater magnificence the wonderful deeds of God.

There are thousands of programs I can imagine, ranging from local history of my own neighborhood all the way to the edge of the universe. Maybe I will begin big (I'm counting on God to have the ultimate in large screens) with the creation of the universe. Since there will be plenty of time (= eternity), I will select the long version, including the formation of the galaxies, the arrangement of the stars, the establishment of the planets and orbits, the creation of life from the most primitive to the most complex.

Sidelight attractions will be information about the much-debated topics: intelligent life in other parts of the universe, flying saucers, the big bang theory.

Events of biblical history will be high on my list. Cecil B. DeMille's *The Ten Commandments* was a good start at reconstructing the Exodus, but there are still many lingering questions about the route, the wandering, and a forty-year diet of manna. I would like to look over Joshua's shoulder at Jericho, watch Samson deal with the Philistines, and listen to the young David play the harp for Saul.

I would like to watch Jesus call the first apostles by the shore of the Sea of Galilee, and see Peter and his friends haul in that surprise catch of fish. I would like to share the joy of the lepers who discovered that they had been healed, and listen to Jesus spin his parables as people gathered around.

I would like to view the development of the area of Subiaco Abbey from prehistoric times, getting a panoramic view of the Indian camps along Cane Creek and the Arkansas River, and learning how our predecessors on this land used the natural environment, making a good life for themselves and leaving plenty for us.

A special treat will be to view the beginnings of Subiaco Abbey itself, watching in full color the early monks and their neighbors I know now only by name and reputation. I've always wanted to look through the hole in the roof where Father Wolfgang Schlumpf saw the stars his first night in bed; and to be with Father Isidore Hobi on his first trip to St. Peter's Chair on the ridges.

I want to watch my family ancestors working through the monumental decisions that brought them from Germany to this country with very little to go on except their faith in God and their confidence in one another. And I would like to learn the other part of the story: how it went for the families who decided to stay where they were.

God's DVD library will have endless other possibilities for viewing; but it also will have one feature to put in a class by itself: after seeing these great and holy people from various centuries on the screen, I will be able to go out into the lobby and meet them in person.

Distractions in Prayer

The biggest rip-off in the history of Western spirituality is the guilt generated by distractions in prayer. As far as the purity of one's prayer goes, involuntary distractions in prayer are extremely unimportant. Prayer is an act of the will. Distractions are loose sparks from the intellect, which cannot affect prayer unless we choose to pursue them.

The preoccupation with mental distractions can be traced back to the French Enlightenment of the eighteenth century. A major thinker of that era, René Descartes, crystallized the attitude of the Enlightenment in the aphorism, *Cogito, ergo sum*, "I think, therefore I am." In other words, a human being is defined by intellectual activity.

A partial truth is always more difficult to detect than a complete error. "I feel, therefore I am" would be an inadequate though partly true statement, because feeling, though a genuine component in human life, is not the whole. But Descartes' choice fell on the characteristic that distinguishes us clearly from other creatures in this world: the ability to reason. As a result, the emotional and intuitive components of our existence, what today we term right-brain functions, were relegated to secondary status; proof of prayer became the purity of the concentration of the mind. Thus involuntary distractions, if not sins, were at least imperfections, and they destroyed the purity of one's prayer.

This concern about the spiritual harm caused by mental distractions has not been an issue in the East, though distractions are just as much a reality to be dealt with there as here. A favorite prayer maxim from the Christian East is "Descend from the mind into the heart." In other words, get beyond ideas to a direct focus on the presence of God. Distractions are interferences that interrupt this focus, but they do not interrupt the prayer itself unless we give in to them and follow them willfully. If the desire to pray remains unbroken, the prayer remains unbroken. The purity of prayer is determined not by the clarity of the focus but by the intensity of the desire.

Typical of the East are images like this from Hindu tradition: "When I sit down to pray it is as if I am under a tree full of monkeys. As soon as I begin my prayer, the monkeys begin to chatter and to swing back and forth to get my attention. Suddenly, I find myself in the tree with the monkeys; as soon as I realize this, I descend to sit under the tree again." This perspective understands that the mind has many levels and that all our other thought processes will not suddenly stop when we decide to pray. But we can descend below our distractions into a deeper level of awareness; when we discover that distractions have pulled us out, we simply return— gently—to the original focus.

This calm attitude toward distractions is evident also in the prayer tradition of the West prior to the Enlightenment. A favorite image St. Teresa of Avila (sixteenth century) used for distractions was what she called *la loca en la casa*, the crazy woman in the house. As she began her prayer the distractions would come, like a visit from a talkative, disturbed neighbor always arriving when she was in the thick of household chores. She would gently turn the distractions away, just as she would ask the woman to come back at a more appropriate time.

Part of the rediscovery of the ancient traditions of prayer in the West, which has been a fruit of the Second Vatican Council, has been a revision of the attitudes that gave too much negative power to involuntary distractions in prayer. Thomas Merton, very influential in this prayer renewal, said simply, "If you have never had any distractions, you don't know how to pray." The solution is not to perform Olympic mental gymnastics to avoid distractions but to find simple ways to return to focus once distractions are noticed (to climb down the tree or send the crazy woman home).

For centuries, the name of Jesus or the Jesus Prayer, psalm verses and gospel sayings, and many different ejaculations have been used as means of focusing attention on God without the need of words. Of special significance to millions is the rosary, which can be used either as a means of meditation on the mysteries of the gospel or simply (as originally) a repetition of Hail Marys as a means of keeping one's attention fixed on the Lord. In either use, the beads are there to help call us back when we find our minds wandering.

One of the saints said that we need distractions to keep us humble in our prayer. They throw us back on the mercy of God and remind us of our weakness. We do not have to fear distractions, which are not limited to prayer but pop into our minds in almost everything we do. Human minds are very lively, and our methods of education train them to be aggressive and inquisitive. It would be strange if we could suddenly turn them off.

There are ways to deal with distractions in prayer and it helps to learn them and use them, but the important thing is to know that prayer is fundamentally a desire of the heart—and as long as that desire is unbroken, whether we are distracted or not, our prayer is unbroken.

A Communion of Intercession

One of the misnomers in our monastic life is the phrase "retired monks." It is a harmless misnomer, but a misnomer nevertheless. Though we speak of retired monks, for example, in the infirmary, that is only an adaptation to the workplace mentality of our society.

Monks never retire from their main work, which is a life of intercession for the world, calling God's blessings of healing and mercy on people everywhere. This life work takes different forms according to the season of one's life. It always means a dedication to the search for God in prayer; but in the physically vigorous years this is coupled with all kinds of work and ministries. The whole life, and not just the prayer, is powerful in bringing blessings, as long as it is focused in the fidelity by which the monks become, in St. Paul's words, "weapons for righteousness" in the hand of God (Rom 6:13).

In some ways the work of a monk intensifies when physical limitations break in. Some of our most active intercessors, in a sense those on the front lines in our mission for the church, are confined to the infirmary or are otherwise restricted by age. At the abbey, these monks form our Senior Prayer Staff, who offer their prayers and sufferings for the needs of the monastery, the church, and the world.

The intercessory vocation is not limited to those who live the monastic life. All of us are called to be channels of blessing to the world according to our particular state. The effectiveness of this work does not diminish with the diminishment of our powers; it may, and often does, increase. I think we need to take another look at the people we consider out of the mainstream because of their limitations and confinement, whether in nursing homes or elsewhere. They may be in the real mainstream.

The ordinary work of this world comes to an end for each of us, but the work of faithful intercession continues. It is not stopped by disease or even by death. This is the remarkable and wonderful truth involved in the doctrine of the communion of saints. Sometimes a person may become mentally impaired by Alzheimer's disease or senility, and may even completely lose rational control. The work of intercession goes on. A pattern of fidelity grows out of a habitual decision of the will, which is not stopped by external circumstances. A comparison may help.

In prayer, though unwanted distractions spoil concentration, they do not automatically interrupt the act of praying. If I return to focus as soon as I notice that I am distracted, the act of prayer, which is an act of the will, remains unbroken. When a faithful person's facilities are impaired, the fidelity remains constant; the decision for God is unbroken, and the intercession continues even though the person has lost contact with mundane reality. I think we see this breaking through in some faithful elderly in nursing homes, who are unable to relate to or understand anything but will suddenly respond to a sign of the cross or join in a Hail Mary.

The work of intercession continues even beyond the grave in the communion of saints. The church calls those who die in Christ the "faithful departed." This is not loose language. They are still faithful, even in death. Death does not, cannot, interrupt fidelity: "For your faithful people, Lord, life is changed, not ended" (Preface for the Faithful Departed).

Our community at Subiaco is much larger than the people listed in our directory. Our brothers who have gone before us in peace are still alive, still engaged in the work of intercession, helping us fulfill the mission to which we have been called. When we encounter various needs in the monastery, the monks ask one another for help and for prayer; but we also call on our older brothers whose bodies rest below the hill in our cemetery. They are still interested in what we are doing, and they are still our faithful intercessors. Our relationships extend much further than the living members.

Besides the gift of continuing intercession, our faithful departed at Subiaco contribute a unique gift to all who come here. They not only continue to pray, but they also continue to preach even from their graves. Visitors to our cemetery often realize that each tombstone represents a faithful life and marks the temporary resting place of a servant of God who remained faithful to his commitment: a man who decided one fine day to dedicate his life by

solemn vows to the Lord and, for better or worse, held out in
faithfulness to the end.

Golden Prayer

Thanks to advances in medical science, people today have
a much longer life expectancy than people who were living
a hundred years ago. This is obviously a great benefit, and
medical researchers will continue to exert themselves to push the
time of death further and further away.

But because human bodies weren't made to last indefinitely in
their present form, the added years may be hard years. "Old age
is not for sissies." Medicine has changed, but the human organism
is still about the same as it was in the time of the psalmist: "Seventy
is the sum of our years, / or eighty, if we are strong" (Ps 90:10).
Our true life is beyond this planet. We are meant to enjoy this
earthly life and live it to the full but not become attached to it or
we might, in the words of St. Gregory, confuse the journey with
the destination.

Longer life in the same old weak bodies has had social effects.
Health care for the elderly is a major national concern. There are
more retirement centers and nursing homes than ever before.
People who have become conditioned to self-sufficiency now find
they are unable to take care of themselves but are reluctant to
become dependent on their families or anyone else. They often
see themselves as useless and in the way.

The church does not see it this way. The church views the wisdom
and holiness of elderly saints as a cumulative treasure gathered
along the way to Jerusalem. Consider Pope John Paul II's words
in *Vita Consecrata* (1996), which explicitly refer to retired religious
but are applicable to all in similar circumstances:

Their witness greatly serves the Church and their own communities, and continues to be worthwhile and meritorious
even when for reasons of age and infirmity they have had to
abandon their specific apostolate. . . . More than in any
activity, the apostolate consists in the witness of one's own
complete dedication to the Lord's saving will, a dedication
nourished by the practice of prayer and penance. (44)

Culturally what makes it difficult for us to avoid the feeling of
inadequacy and uselessness in the years of physical decline, even
in the church, is the exaltation of function over being. What I do
is more important than who I am.

But life is not just a series of actions. Life is the journey that
gives unity and direction to our deeds. The true direction of a life
is not revealed immediately, and it is usually not established immediately. A Christian life is a journey of faith that reveals itself
over time. Those who are true to this calling bring grace to the
world not only by what they do but also by what they are, in fact,
perhaps more by what they are.

God has chosen to save and sanctify the world by the mysterious
process called "incarnation," in which divine grace flows through
human persons. We are "in Christ," the definitive incarnation of
God. Our call in Christ is to become open channels of blessing for
the world by making ourselves more and more available for God's
action in and through us.

This is ordinarily not a quick process but is the work of years.
People committed to this journey develop a pattern of life in which
their work and prayer lead them more and more to simplicity of
focus. They come to know what is important and what isn't. They
overcome the habit of compartmentalizing life into isolated spheres
of work, rest, prayer, meals, visiting, worship, and recreation. All
becomes one.

Faithful disciples who have come to the golden years grow into
a state of prayer. This does not mean they think of God all the
time, but their life is focused in God. By grace and suffering, they

have been emptied of egoism, hollowed out to become channels of blessing. Though they have concern for everyone and everything that is going on, they have no great plans or demands but by their lives are pleading to God in constant intercession.

Of people like this Thomas Merton wrote: "They are the tabernacles of God in the world; they are the ones who keep the universe from being destroyed; they are the little ones; they do not know themselves, but the whole earth depends on them."

On the face of it this is a very extravagant statement. But those who pray daily know enough of the effect of prayer to begin to imagine the incredible extent of what lies beyond their knowledge. Most of us live as if reality is coextensive with what we see and experience with our senses. But the saints know that the visible reality is only a crumb compared to the vast unseen world surrounding us.

For these faithful ones, the time of retirement means anything but inactivity. Physical exertion may diminish to a standstill, but the inner work intensifies. It is beyond experience, but it is real.

Even those who lose their mental faculties in the extremities of Alzheimer's disease are still interceding for the world. When practicing Catholics are unconscious from an accident we administer the sacrament of anointing, presuming on their "habitual intention" to receive whatever the church offers. A prayerful person who has entered the zone of mental incompetence likewise remains in a habitual attitude of prayer, unbroken by the failure of health. The heart that has chosen by free human decisions over years to be emptied of self and filled with Christ remains fixed in that attitude and continues as a channel of God's grace for the world.

Spiritual ministry does not end when age and disability require retirement from activities. It moves to a new level of humble availability, an "apostolate of complete dedication to the Lord's saving will" (Pope John Paul II), through which untold benefits come to the church and the world.

The Usefulness of Monasteries

In 1835 almost all the monasteries in Spain were closed by the government and their properties were taken over for national needs. More than 20,000 men and women religious were evicted, many with no place to go but the streets. The same thing was happening in other European countries on various scales in a great wave of secularization, and it continued into the twentieth century in some places.

There was only one way a religious house could preserve itself: by showing its usefulness to the state and to society. The government allowed some religious houses to continue in existence if their members worked in schools and hospitals. But all the communities devoted mainly to prayer were suppressed. They served no useful purpose.

People of faith see the world quite differently than this. We concede that work in schools and hospitals is important, as well as all kinds of hands-on service to human needs. But to focus exclusively on what can be seen is to lose touch with the context, to distort, to confuse a part of reality with the whole. This world is part of a larger reality, the meaning and purpose of which cannot be discerned through a merely secular perspective. What is required is the perspective of the world's creator, of God.

Over a century and a half after the trouble in Spain, monasteries are still a curiosity, but mostly undisturbed. What they are up to is not often any clearer to governments than before. And because all but the most enclosed monasteries do some form of visible service in the world, their purpose and impact may continue to be judged on that level.

At Subiaco Abbey in Arkansas we conduct a school, minister in parishes, give retreats and hospitality, raise quality cattle, and do various other things which can be seen as contributions and services to society. Maybe with this we could have avoided suppression in the 1800s. But while these are all good works, we do not understand them as standing on their own. They are not why we are here. They are the overflow or the outflow of our community life of seeking God.

Recently we have sought ways to emphasize the role of prayer in our relationship with others, to make prayer itself more vividly a sign and seal of our communion. About five years ago we began more systematically to keep track of the prayer requests we receive from our friends, to post them on our community bulletin board and to include them in the intentions at Vespers, our final community prayer of the day. We established a Prayer Hotline to make it easier for people to contact us with personal issues and prayer requests. Since that time the hotline (1-800-350-5889) has been open to receive calls 24 hours every day, and a monk is available from 6:30 p.m. to 7:00 p.m. daily to respond personally and to monitor the calls that have come in.

As important as we feel this kind of contact is, our communion in prayer goes much deeper. We are praying for people's needs—in fact, the needs of the church and world—every time we come together for the "prayer of the Church," the Liturgy of the Hours, and whenever we come before God individually in personal prayer. Monastic life emphasizes the conviction of the church that even prayer completely alone and in silence, including prayer without words, is always intercessory beyond our awareness.

No one has expressed this communion of prayer more beautifully than St. Paul at the beginning of his letter to his friends at Philippi: "I give thanks to my God at every remembrance of you, praying always with joy in my every prayer for all of you, because of your partnership in the gospel from the first day until now. . . . I hold you in my heart, you who are all partners with me in grace" (Phil 1:3-5, 7).

Why Monasticism?

The Second Vatican Council said of monastic contemplative life that it "should be restored everywhere, because it
belongs to the fullness of the Church's presence" (Decree
on the Church's Missionary Activity, 18). Though it is the oldest
type of religious life and is highly respected, the monastic vocation
is not well understood. Probably this is due to the rise and pre-
dominance during recent centuries of the "active" orders, with
which monasticism is usually associated and in the light of which
it is often judged.

People often think of our monastery as a gathering place for
church ministers: a pool of resources where priests and brothers
receive training, pray together, and mutually support one another
for the active work of the church. This certainly describes a dimension of our life, but it misses the point of our vocation. The misunderstanding is most clearly revealed when someone asks a fully
professed brother, "Why don't you go all the way and be ordained?"
In a monastery, a member who has made solemn profession,
ordained or not, has gone "all the way." All of us are primarily
brothers, even those who have been ordained.

Monasticism is mainly a vocation to a life of prayer. What makes
it hard to comprehend is that our religious atmosphere is domi-
nated by a limited notion of prayer. I am not speaking about any
impoverishment of prayer in the teaching of the church, where a
rich, authentic understanding of prayer has been passed down
through the various spiritual traditions and is celebrated in the
liturgy. But the general mood of the time concerning prayer is
quite different and the common understanding of prayer much
narrower.

The familiar catechism acronym ACTS identifies the elements
of authentic prayer as Adoration, Contrition, Thanksgiving, and
Supplication. All of these are present in the Mass, as they are in
most ritual prayers. But people who pray very little will usually

focus on a single element, supplication. Another word for this is begging, the lowest common denominator of prayer, the kind of prayer that spontaneously arises in all of us in time of need: in the face of war, or the danger of cancer, or an important exam, or financial pressure.

There is nothing wrong with this kind of prayer in its proper context; but when prayer is only this, it is not much different from operating a slot machine, rejoicing when it delivers a jackpot and banging and kicking when it fails to respond. Begging prayer isolated from other prayers is only an occasional blip on the screen of our life, more superstitious than relational. Its prevalence is what makes prayer seem marginal and naive to many people.

Growth in the spiritual life brings a maturing in prayer. The more we pray, the more we integrate the various parts and turn more naturally to the higher types, adoration and thanksgiving, which are also more oriented away from ourselves and toward God. God, in fact, becomes a personal presence rather than a mental image or a last resort for difficulties. And the conviction of God's constant loving concern frees us to develop a profound sense of the intercessory character of all prayer. For when I open myself to God's presence, besides being warmed and healed by grace, I find myself present in God to the whole world and the needs of all his people. By the incarnation of his Son, God has forged links between all his children, and by God's mysterious design, he uses my availability in faith, my love, to bless them. I may express my petition or not: he knows and acts.

Some years ago, I was struck by the words of Anglican Archbishop Desmond Tutu of South Africa. In a sermon at the National Cathedral in Washington DC, he thanked Christians of the world for their prayers for his suffering people and said, "Sometimes you may not feel like praying because your prayers are insipid, because there is a dryness and God seems miles and miles away. But because you are faithful, you say to God: 'I want to pray, and I offer you these thirty minutes even if it means fighting these awkward distractions.' And because of your faithfulness, someone in a prison cell in South Africa receives an excess of grace; inexplicably, it appears." He gave the example of someone in the midst of torture being able to see in the one torturing a misguided child of God in need of love. This gift of grace, he said, comes from your prayer.

Archbishop Tutu was not simply thanking people who "remembered South Africa in their prayers." He was also making a deeper connection between the personal prayer of believers throughout the world and the gifts of grace bestowed in South Africa. He was thinking not only of those who consciously remembered South Africa, but all who were faithful to prayer.

This is where monasticism comes in. Monasticism is a way of life focusing on the prayer reality that is part of every life of genuine faith. Its symbolic center is choir prayer, which the Rule of St. Benedict calls the Work of God: "Nothing is to be preferred to the Work of God." Whether in choir or privately, at work or at leisure, whether with specific petitions and intentions or an unspecific openness to God, monks make themselves available to God for the sake of the world. The church depends on them for many things, but mainly for this. When one of the first monks, St. Pachomius, was asked the reason for his monastic life of prayer, he answered simply: "I have become a monk to save mankind."

Some monasteries, like ours, also serve people directly through various ministries. We believe that, in our particular vocation, the spiritual energy for these ministries flows from the prayer life at the heart of our community—and so we see it as vital to our calling to maintain that strength at the center. Critics of our way of life say that we would help the world more if we could scatter ourselves to serve more of the world's crying needs. But we believe that by doing that we would do less, that we could never do directly what the church depends on us to do indirectly through our community life of prayer. By our personal contact and involvement we would reach hundreds more, a wonderful thing, but not the millions the church depends on us to reach every day through prayer.

The Family of Jesus

The pilgrimage shrine of the Black Christ in Esquipulas, Guatemala, is ministered to by the monks of the local Benedictine Abbey of Jesucristo Crucificado (Jesus Christ Crucified). The focal point is the crucifix with a black corpus that dates back to 1595. Pope John Paul II visited the shrine on the occasion of its four hundredth anniversary. What impresses me (and probably all visitors) is the intense fervor and dedication of the pilgrims, some of whom walk for miles and even days to spend time at the shrine, often in family groups. People from the United States, however, are not always ready for some of the ways the pilgrims at Esquipulas express their devotion. (The same is true at the shrine of Our Lady of Guadalupe in Mexico City, which is more frequently the destination of U.S. travelers.) But during my visit to the abbey, it gradually dawned on me what was really happening.

The Esquipulas basilica is a cavernous eighteenth-century building, with a high ceiling and a large nave with movable pews covering only a small part of the dark pavement floor. Scattered throughout the church on pilgrimage days are small groups of worshipers gathered around the flickering candles they have placed on the pavement. The light and smoke from the candles create a subdued reverential atmosphere. The smoke also causes a grayness to settle on the white walls.

Guatemalan families save throughout the year to be able to make their annual pilgrimage and to be able to stay at the shrine from one to several days. Often they will establish a family spot on the floor of the basilica. There they will set up their candles, deposit food and clothing that will be needed, and begin to spend time in the Divine Presence. They will participate in Mass when it is offered, pray the rosary with a group or silently at other times, go forward to pay special reverence to the Black Christ, or simply sit in silence. They go in and out of the basilica during the day to eat, relax, to have their rosaries and images blessed, to have their families sprinkled with holy water.

What may disconcert a U.S. visitor is the way that, when they are not focused on a particular prayer or worship, the pilgrims will also doze at their spot in church, or whisper to one another, or get up and wander around, or play with their children. In short, they don't act as if they're in church; they act as if they are at home.

That's the point that finally got through my skull. These pilgrims are not going into foreign territory when they enter the basilica. They are members of the family of Jesus, and this is their home. They can relax and be themselves. They are comfortable just being in the presence of God their father, Jesus their brother, and the Lady of Guadalupe their mother.

In Arkansas and many other parts of our country, we are welcoming large numbers of Hispanic Catholics from the countries south of us. Every day we are discovering in new ways what a treasure this is. Pope Benedict XVI and other recent popes have reminded us that the church is blessed and enriched by the gifts the various cultures bring to Christian life and worship. We can learn from one another as our cultures come together.

I think I discovered in the pilgrim groups at Esquipulas and Guadalupe one important gift our Hispanic brothers and sisters are bringing to us: that coming into God's house is coming into our house. Catholics in the mainstream white U.S. culture, with our roots in central Europe, have been raised with a more formal approach to prayer and worship, which has gifted the church in many ways with ordered beauty. As African American Catholics are reclaiming their heritage and bringing it into more prominence in the church, they are beginning to bring to others their creative gifts of freedom and joy in worship. Now we are becoming aware of the special gifts of Hispanic Catholics, and one of these is comfortable intimacy in the family of Jesus.

This way of worshiping leaves some loose ends, the same as life in a busy family. There may be delays, sick babies, slip-ups in planning.

But the main thing is to be with the family, in this case God's family, to spend time in the divine Presence together. Words are helpful but not always needed. Silence communicates too; the right kind of silence sets a contemplative atmosphere. Hours go by in the basilica at Esquipulas when some individuals don't seem to be doing anything. What we might learn is that just being there is doing something.

Private Revelations

When Father Benedict J. Groeschel, CFR, was here at the abbey to preach a retreat for diocesan priests some years ago, he gave a conference on the place of private devotions in the church. He saw the need to help the priests refresh their seminary training on the topic because of the increasing reports of Marian apparitions and private revelations at the present time.

Later he prepared the information for wider distribution in a small book, *A Still, Small Voice: A Practical Guide on Reported Revelations*. Father Groeschel himself has a devotion to Our Lady of Lourdes, and he has been interested in the happenings at Medjugorje. During a pilgrimage to Medjugorje, he interviewed one of the visionaries, Maria Pavrovich, for an hour and reported that he was impressed by her level-headed and sensible attitude toward her experiences.

Father Groeschel's concern is neither to promote nor to discourage interest in the reported apparitions at these and other places, but to help Catholics situate these phenomena properly within the overall context of Catholic belief and practice. Without proper guidance, believers can fall into extremes of skepticism or credulity.

He organizes his presentation around several norms gleaned from church instructions:

1. Private revelations have no significance apart from the public revelation of Scripture and tradition. "Do you want to know a certain and direct revelation of God? Pick up a Bible and read it! Do you want to be speedily and mysteriously in the presence of Christ? Reverently and prayerfully visit the Blessed Sacrament!" This will give you a sound framework for assessing later reported revelations.

2. No private revelation can be assumed to be without error, because it is always filtered through the human facilities of the recipient. It must always be evaluated in the light of public revelation. The experience may be true and the report still inaccurate, not because of ill will but because of weakness. Saint Catherine Labouré, for example, simply apologized for getting the details of her revelation wrong when some of her historical predictions proved false.

3. Even revelations that have been approved, such as those at Lourdes or Fatima, "ought not to, and cannot receive from us an assent of Catholic or divine faith, but only human faith, according to the rules of prudence" (Pope Benedict XIV). Divine faith may be given only to public revelation; other events and messages are subject to the usual norms of practical judgment.

4. A private revelation by definition is intended for and binding only on the person (or persons) for whom it is intended.

Then what is the purpose of apparitions and private revelations? They are divine encouragements to guide and reassure individuals or, in particular cases, even the whole church. They serve in much the same way as private spiritual devotions, which encourage personal renewal, prayer, and conversion of heart. Through them the light of the one gospel is split into rainbow colors for different cultures and personalities, and for the particular needs of a time or place.

But they are encouragements, not commands. It is good to share devotions and private revelations with others, as an offer to enrich their spiritual lives, but it is a mistake to force them on people as essential to salvation, or to treat them as if they are on the same level as the sacramental system and public revelation.

Both private revelations and private devotions will eventually be judged by the effect they produce in the people of God in our time; authenticity will be marked by a movement of conversion, prayer, and charity, works of justice and peace, and a deepening of sacramental participation and community life in the church.

A Rock to Cling To

Four days after the terrorist attacks of September 11, 2001, I left the abbey to give a retreat at a monastery of Benedictine women. Unlike the experience of thousands of people, my immediate plans were not disrupted by the tragic events of that day, and so I was able to carry through with what I had originally planned.

Much had changed, though. Terrorism was flooding the media and was on everyone's mind. Commentators said immediately that as a result of the attack our country would never be the same, and they were undoubtedly right in the sense that we will never feel as secure within our borders as we did before September 11.

I knew it was a providential time to be on retreat, but only afterward did I comprehend the gift of spending the first days after the attack in a community of faith. In some places it must have seemed that the ground underneath our feet had forever shifted and the rules had changed. It was a soul-searching time. Many were bewildered and shaken. Others had a profound spiritual awakening when confronted with a collapse of their foundations.

But in those days of retreat, though the same news and commentary were in free circulation at the monastery as everywhere else, I experienced a deep sense of calm in the community on retreat. Things had changed, but not the important things, not the realities on the basis of which this group of women had committed their lives. This was a monumental tragedy that called forth a response of love and concern, compassion and prayer. But it was not "unexpected" in a world our faith tells us is "groaning in labor pains" (Rom 8:22) until the victory of Christ is complete.

Faith, however, can be blind, uninformed, and misguided (we need look no further than the terrorists themselves). During that time of tragedy, it helped to be supported by a solid faith tradition forged out of the experience of centuries. There was no danger of facile solutions or dictates about the meaning of the crisis or responses to it, nor was there the danger of scapegoating certain nationalities or religions that might come from a faith responding in a historical or moral vacuum.

Our faith also gave us a way to respond, to do something about the crisis personally. We were not able to join the heroic rescue workers or those providing hands-on help around the clock to people impacted by the tragedy. But there was something we were already dedicated to by our baptism and by our monastic vows, and that linked us intimately with people of faith all around the world: we could pray.

That is easy to say and at times may seem like an escape. We don't know what else to say, so we say, "I'll pray for you." Granted it can be a dodge, but it doesn't have to be; and a misuse or failure doesn't negate the reality. Jesus invites us to ask, seek, and knock, and by God's own design he works through us in this world. We don't even have to know what is best or what to ask for; what God needs is suppliant hearts.

All those who have committed their lives to God received a call to the frontline of prayer on September 11. Not so much to prayers for certain intentions or specific persons, though that practice is one wonderful way, but to the daily gift of ourselves to God on the altar of our heart, however we do it. Often it is in simple silence. We prostrate ourselves interiorly before God for the sake of the world and ask God to use our hearts as channels for good wherever needed. Our faith tells us that is enough. In the words of *The Cloud of Unknowing*, a spiritual classic from fourteenth-century England:

> One loving blind desire for God alone is more valuable in itself, more pleasing to God and to the saints, more beneficial to your own growth, and more helpful to your friends, both living and dead, than anything else you could do.

We cannot do everything to respond to international crises, but we can pray, and who knows if it is not the most important thing?

The American Dream

Two books published within the past decade have a lot to say about the true nature of the American Dream. Both focus on the momentous events of April 1865 as the Civil War ended and Abraham Lincoln was assassinated. The books are *April 1865: The Month That Saved America* by Jay Winik and *Lincoln's Greatest Speech: The Second Inaugural* by Ronald C. White Jr.

Winik shows how three people in the divided leadership acted in an unexpected way at a critical moment. He maintains that if they had followed the more traveled road that leadership takes in such times, we would probably be two or more nations today instead of the United States. The lead was given by Lincoln, followed by Ulysses S. Grant for the North, and, incredibly, responded to by

Robert E. Lee for the South. These three men were interested not in vengeance or personal gain but in the good of all the people. Lincoln and Grant insisted that the vanquished Confederates be treated with respect, as brothers instead of enemies; and Lee, when others were clamoring to continue the fight by guerilla warfare (and thus also to keep himself from being humbled), knew that this would simply deepen the wound of suffering America, making it impossible to heal. These men rose above themselves and sought true peace for the future of the nation. Each drew strength from the others. Later Lee would say he surrendered "as much to Lincoln's goodness as to Grant's armies."

White identifies as Lincoln's greatest speech not the Gettysburg Address but the Second Inaugural Address, given at the moment when the victory of the Union was assured, only a few days before Lincoln's death. All expected a rousing victory speech, a lesson for the Confederacy, a message of right on our side and wrong on yours, crowing and strutting. Instead Lincoln reached for the heart of the divided nation, seeing all as one people, and realizing that the greatest need at the moment was to seek reconciliation and healing, not more condemnation and blame. He ended his address with the famous words:

> With malice toward none, with charity for all, with firmness in the right, as God gives us to see the right, let us strive on to finish the work we are in, to bind up the nation's wounds; to care for him who shall have borne the battle, and for his widow, and his orphan, to do all which may achieve and cherish a lasting peace among ourselves, and with all nations.

This turned out to be his legacy to the nation, for a few days later he was dead.

We live in a time of terror, and we do not know whether the threat to our future is greater now than it was in April 1865, but the stakes have been raised because the threat is not only within our borders but also worldwide. Our place in the world has changed, and now we have a responsibility for the future of the whole world. What will the world be like in the next century? Will people look back to our time in gratitude because our leaders responded to crisis with the kind of vision and humanity that was exhibited in 1865? Or will our generation be seen as responsible for wreckage?

The leaders in 1865 were able to distinguish between fighting for a cause and fighting against an enemy. The only reason that the North and South were enemies was because they were fighting for different causes, and each stood in the other's way. The soldiers were not naturally enemies, but brothers. As the war dragged on, it became harder and harder for most people to keep this in mind. Lincoln did, though, and as soon as it became clear which cause would triumph, he used all his authority to reconcile the divided family, "with malice toward none, with charity for all." Much of the subsequent suffering and hostility in postwar America could have been avoided if the architects of Reconstruction had followed Lincoln's lead. But once he was gone, not many could hold the high ground.

Our passion for a cause must not obliterate our love for all God's children, no matter where they stand, even if they stand in the way of what is right, "as God gives us to see the right." Sometimes war is necessary to establish and preserve the true good of all, even the vanquished. If it is not for that purpose, it can never be just. It is then, like abortion, just getting people out of our way.

Abraham Lincoln, Ulysses S. Grant, and Robert E. Lee were locked in a monumental struggle with the future of the nation at risk. They were able to rise above self-interest and national drum-beating and act for the common good. They were all capable of the brilliant maneuver, but what saved the country came to humility and to love, even love of the enemy. Lucky for us, they were also capable of that. Now the future of the world is at risk. Emulating Lincoln, Grant, and Lee is a healthy challenge, but is it too much to ask our present leaders to give it a try? Can't we still Dream?